EAT &
EXPLORE
Oklahoma

Cookbook & Travel Guide

EAT &

EXPLORE

Oklahoma

Cookbook & Travel Guide

by Christy Campbell

Great American Publishers

www.GreatAmericanPublishers.com

TOLL-FREE 1.888.854.5954

Recipe Collection © 2012 by Great American Publishers

Great American Publishers

171 Lone Pine Church Road • Lena, MS 39094

TOLL-FREE 1.888.854.5954 • www.GreatAmericanPublishers.com

ISBN 978-1-934817-11-7

10 9 8 7 6 5 4

by Christy Campbell

Front cover: National Route 66 Museum © City of Elk City; Chuckwagon cooking: © Western Spirit Celebration p81; Iron skillet chili: istockphoto © MSPhotographic
Back cover festival image: Pops in Arcadia p227; Sopapillas © TheCrimsonMonkey, istockphoto.com

Chapter opening photos, istockphoto.com: Appetizers & Beverages © Smokingdrum; Soups, Salads & Breads © funwithfood; Vegetables & Side Dishes © Diana Didyk; Meat & Seafood © Ezhicheg; Desserts & Other Sweets © Edward ONeil Photography; Indexes © Nancy Nehring

Pages: Woodward Main Street p15 ©John McMahon/Woodward News; Blue Whale of Catoosa p25 © Brad Nickson, Catoosa Arts & Tourism Society; Turner Falls Park p29 ©Buck Bridges, www.oklahomahistory.net; Billy Boy BBQ p52 © Mika Designs; Paul's Place Steakhouse p53 © Mika Designs; Turnip Festival p105 © Karen Eckhardt; Soda Fountain Eatery p187 © Annata78/Dreamstime.com; Cimarron River Stampede Rodeo p203 © Mark Carson; The Meers Store and Restaurant p221 © Jerry Russell, www.cbsop.com.jpg

Pages, istockphoto.com: Background © DavidMSchrader; covered wagon p2 © dmfoss; Wheat field p6 © dmfoss; Spinach and artichoke dip p16 © Jochel28; Buffalo chicken dip p20 © 1MoreCreative; Watermelon salsa p26 © bhofack2; Winter's Day au Lait p38 © barol16; Lemonade p42 © Lecic; Potato soup p48 © David Pimborough; Rodeo clowns p70 © dgphotography; Green beans p92 © HandmadePictures; Squash p102 © Azurita; Quiche p112 © margouillatphotos; Four-wheeler p120 © sculpies; Meatballs p168 © kabVisio; Pecan pie p204 © msheldrake; Snickerdoodles p212 © SouthernLightStudios; Oatmeal-raisin cookies p216 © Joel Albrizio; Fudge p232 © Andrea Mink

Contents

Introduction

Before beginning this journey through Oklahoma, my perspective of the state was typical: Cowboys, Native Americans, Route 66 and oil. My, how that has changed! Rich traditions spanning generations are alive and well in this colorful state, and the state pride felt by its citizens is evident in every endeavor. Things I'm sure I learned long ago in grade school were brought into the forefront of my mind, and now each bit of information has been added to the tapestry of America's history I've begun to weave. The Oklahoma Land Run of 1889 was a remarkable event, and envisioning families desperately racing to grab a piece of land to call their own is beyond imagination. Learning the history of Historic Route 66 and how it holds a special place in the American story, enlightened me to our love affair with the automobile. I learned of the internal structure of many Native American Nations, the importance of the Chisholm Trail, and how Oklahoma became one of the largest gas and oil producing states in the nation.

The landscape of Oklahoma is as varied as its history, ranging from rolling hills to high plains. Opportunities for trail rides, hunting, fishing and hiking are available throughout the state and the sites are beautiful. And those "amber waves of grain" boasted in the famous song? Oklahoma has them. Wheat is one of the main crops produced in Oklahoma, in addition to corn, maize and potatoes.

Which leads me to the heart and soul of this journey … the food. As each recipe came to my desk, I would exclaim to my husband "I have something to try for dinner!" **Grandma's Corn Casserole, Indian Tacos**, **Chuck Wagon Sourdough Bread** and **Kim and Bob's Hot Coffee Steak** are Oklahoma favorites that are a must for any meal. The savory delights continue with even more tried and true favorites like **Sicilian Sweet Spaghetti Sauce**, **Fabulous Macaroni and Cheese** and **Mom's Chicken Salad**. And I can't leave out the desserts! Goodness, there were so many wonderful sweets, but I had no trouble at all trying them out. **Coconut-Caramel Pie**, **Sopapillas** and **Chocolatey Raspberry Crumb Bars** are always a hit. Then there are twists on old favorites like **Root Beer Bread Pudding**, **Pumpkin Italian Cream Cake**, **Bailey's Croissants** and **Spiced and Iced Pumpkin Cookies**. If I learned anything at all during the time spent putting together this cookbook, it's that Oklahomans certainly know good food.

As the team at Great American Publishers expands and grows, each person's contribution to our ultimate goal must be recognized. I want to say a very special thank you to Brooke Craig, my new upstairs office mate and the most insightful leader into what makes things tick. Her input into the Eat & Explore State Cookbook Series is something we simply could not do without. What would I do without Leann Crapps? Well, I certainly wouldn't have anyone to borrow books from, that's for sure, and I also wouldn't have a valuable asset to my sales endeavors. Krista Griffin's opinion and viewpoints are hidden treasures waiting to be discovered, and the amazing efforts of Krista and Jayme McMorris keep us going strong. Roger Simmons, aka Santa Claus, will always be the grounding voice. My fellow couponer Leslie Shoemaker helps gives us a presence in the world, and Noel Waggoner's tenacity is the thing that keeps it all going. And we're waiting on the return of our favorite new Mom, Lacy Fikes. I'm ready to see her welcoming smile.

What to say about Sheena Steadham, Heather Bowman and Christy Jenkins? There are not enough words to express the sincere gratitude and appreciation to their work on the Eat & Explore State Cookbook Series. Sheena's sincerity and Heather's enthusiasm are positive attributes that have helped us grow, and Christy's sense of humor and knowledge are greatly missed.

It is fitting to round out the accolades with Sheila Simmons. Her professionalism, knowledge, generosity and talent are unparalleled. Sheila, thank you for each day I get to work with you, each one is a gift and a blessing. Last but not least are the boys … Michael, Michael-Jason and Preston, get ready, I'm taking you to Oklahoma in the summer.

The second leg of Eat & Explore's winding trail through America's traditions brought me to The Sooner State, and I am most grateful to the people of Oklahoma for sharing their traditions and celebrations. Once again, I look forward to seeing each and every one of you as the journey continues, and until then, have fun exploring … Oklahoma.

Chris Cpbell

Appetizers & Beverages

Party Mix

2 cups Corn Chex
2 cups Rice Chex
2 cups Wheat Chex
1 can mixed nuts

1 can french fried onions
¼ cup melted butter
2 tablespoons brown sugar
1 tablespoon steak seasoning

Combine cereal, nuts and onions in large mixing bowl; mix. Add butter, brown sugar and steak seasoning; mix well. Microwave 6 minutes, stirring every 2 minutes. Spread on cookie sheet to cool.

Jane Apple
Hitching Post Bed & Breakfast

Fruit Pizza

½ tube sugar cookie dough
4 ounces cream cheese,
  softened

2 tablespoons powdered sugar
4 ounces Cool Whip
Fruit for topping

Spread cookie dough on greased pizza pan or cookie sheet. Bake according to package directions and cool. Mix cream cheese, powdered sugar, and Cool Whip. Spread onto cooled cookie crust. Top with kiwi, strawberries, pineapple, bananas or fruit of choice.

Jane Apple
Hitching Post Bed & Breakfast

Hitching Post Bed & Breakfast

101 South Cimarron and HCR 1 Box 4 • 3½ miles East of Kenton
580-261-7413 • blackmesacountry.wordpress.com

The Hitching Post Bed & Breakfast and cabins are located on the Old 101 Ranch which was in operation in the mid-1800s. Jane Apple's granddad came to work on the 101 Ranch in 1886. It was later owned by Jane's parents. The Apples now own the ranch and run mama cows with calves to brand and cows to move. They still do their cattle work by horseback. Fourteen years ago the Apples made one of the ranch houses into a bed & breakfast. Today they have two additional cabins. This is the perfect spot to get away and rest in the beauty of creation, for hiking, or watching birds all while visiting a historical site. There are trail rides and overnight campouts available, and guests may bring their own horse.

Great hunting – good cooking…. Come to the Hitching Post.

Caramel Corn

7 quarts popped popcorn
2 cups brown sugar
2 sticks butter
½ teaspoon baking soda
1 teaspoon salt
1 teaspoon vanilla

Preheat oven to 300°. Boil sugar and butter 5 minutes. Add baking soda, salt and vanilla. Mix with popped corn. Bake in large pan 1 hour, stirring occasionally.

Karolyn Anders
Holiday in the Park

Toasted Squash Seeds

Squash seeds
Seasoned salt to taste

Rinse seeds in cold water and rub off the outer tissue. Rinse again and drain. Spread seeds evenly on cookie sheet and sprinkle with seasoned salt. Bake at 350° for 15 to 20 minutes.

Harn Homestead & 1889ers Museum

Firecrackers

1 box (4 sleeves) ZESTA crackers
1⅓ cups Canola oil
1 package dry ranch dressing mix
3 tablespoons red pepper flakes (4 tablespoons if you like it
  hotter)

Empty crackers in 2-gallon Ziplock bag. In a separate bowl, mix oil, dry dressing mix and pepper flakes thoroughly. Pour over crackers. Seal bag. Turn and toss to coat crackers. Let stand 12 hours, turning periodically. Remove crackers from bag and place in dry container for storage.

Dixie Clement
Chisholm Trail Historical Preservation Society, Inc.

Dill Weed Crackers

1 box (4 sleeves) ZESTA crackers
1⅓ cups Canola oil
1 package dry ranch dressing mix
3 to 4 tablespoons cracked dill weed

Empty crackers in 2-gallon Ziplock bag. Mix oil, dry dressing mix and dill weed thoroughly. Pour over crackers. Seal bag. Turn and toss to coat crackers. Let stand 12 hours, turning periodically. Remove crackers from bag and place in dry container for storage.

Dixie Clement
Chisholm Trail Historical Preservation Society, Inc.

Spiced Pretzels

¾ cup oil or olive oil
1 package dry ranch dressing
   mix
1 teaspoon cayenne pepper

1 teaspoon lemon pepper
1 teaspoon garlic salt
1 large bag small pretzels

In large bowl, mix all ingredients, except pretzels. Add pretzels then stir until all oil is absorbed. Place on wax paper or paper towel and spread out to dry. Eat and enjoy.

Kim West
Woodward Main Street

Come Home to Woodward

Photo by Scott Starns

Woodward Main Street

1102 Main Street
Downtown Woodward
580-254-8521
www.woodwardmainstreet.net

The unique charm and personality of Woodward has an appeal worth preserving, and Main Street Woodward is honored to take part in this creative effort.

Woodward is a terrific community, and its dedicated business owners partner with the Main Street program to support a number of projects and events. Preservation and revitalization is the focus, and downtown Woodward is a shining example of the fruits of effort and commitment.

In addition the progress in the downtown district, Main Street Woodward is proud to sponsor many events for the community. Westfest is the place to be in September! The main stage is the epicenter of the action, complete with the cutest cowgirl and cowboy contest, live music, a talent and dance contest, hot pepper eating contest, hot dog eating contest, and the stiletto race. Westfest grows year after year, and so does the fun. The kid's have their fair share of fun – there are awesome games, balloon artists, tractor races, caricature artists, jump jumps and more. The festivities last from morning till sundown.

Contact Main Street Woodward to find out more about events and developments in the downtown area.

Warm Spinach and Artichoke Dip

1½ cups sour cream
8 to 16 ounces cream cheese
1 or 2 packages frozen spinach, thawed, drained and squeezed dry
1 (6.5-ounce) jar artichoke hearts, drained and chopped
1½ cups Parmesan cheese, separated
1 can water chestnuts, chopped
Garlic salt, cayenne pepper, salt, pepper and red pepper flakes to taste

Mix all ingredients using 1 cup Parmesan cheese and place in a casserole dish. Sprinkle remaining ½ cup Parmesan cheese on top. Bake at 350° for 35 to 40 minutes until bubbly. I buy the artichoke hearts in seasoned brine and add a little of the juice for more flavor.

Sondra Martin
Bedstead Retreat

Bedstead Retreat

Hwy 259 North Battiest Road • Bethel
580-241-5347 • www.bedsteadretreat.com

Escape to Southeast Oklahoma's scenic beauty and enjoy the spectacular views of the hills and streams of McCurtain County.

Situated on 40 acres of hardwood property in the Sherwood Community of Northern McCurtain County, the Bedstead Retreat cabin offers a view of Hee Mountain and nature at its best. It is just 7½ miles to Broken Bow Lake via the McCurtain County Wilderness Area Road, and 13½ miles to the Upper Mountain Fork River (The Narrows). It is also within 20 minutes of Beaver's Bend State Park, Cedar Creek Golf Course, National Forest land, and Glover River.

The location is perfect for a romantic getaway or provides ample opportunities for hunting, fishing, ATV's, and hiking.

Hot Cheese Olive Dip

4 ounces grated Cheddar cheese
4 ounces grated mozzarella cheese
1 bunch green onions, chopped
½ cup chopped green olives
¾ cup chopped ripe olives
1 cup Hellmann's mayonnaise

Mix all in glass pie plate. Bake 20 minutes at 350°.
Serve with tortilla chips.

Courtesy of Santa's Old Broads
Pelican Festival

Santa's Old Broads

Santa's Old Broads provide Christmas for disadvantaged children in the Grove area. Selling their *Doing It in the Kitchen* cookbooks raises money needed for this annual project. They can be found at: www.santasoldbroads.com and on Facebook.

Pelican Festival

Fourth Weekend in September

Civic Center • Grove
918-786-2289 • www.grandlakefun.com

The Pelican Festival is one of NE Oklahoma's most unique events. The festival honors the Great White American Pelican that migrates to Grand Lake each September in large numbers and stays for several months before they continue south.

The Pelican Festival consists of a carnival with rides and games for all ages, an arts and crafts fair, kids games, musical entertainment, and pelican tours around Grand Lake on the world famous Cherokee Queen. On Saturday there is free admission to the Historic Har-Ber Village.

There is also the crowd favorite, the Pelican Festival Parade on Saturday morning. Each float has have to have some sort of Pelican design on display.

The Pelican Festival is held at the Grove Civic Center and it is a great event for the whole family.

Buffalo Chicken Dip

1 (8-ounce) package cream cheese, softened
2 cans chunk white chicken breast
½ cup Texas Pete hot sauce
½ cup blue cheese salad dressing
½ cup crumbled blue cheese

Preheat oven to 350°. Mix together all ingredients until well blended. Pour into casserole dish and bake 20 minutes. Serve with vegetables or crackers.

Kiamichi Outdoor Sportsman's Festival

Kiamichi Outdoor Sportsman's Festival

First Weekend in September

Dewey Avenue • Downtown Poteau
918-647-8648 • www.poteaumainstreetmatters.com

Come to Poteau and discover why Eastern Oklahomans are some of the luckiest people in the world. This area of the state is perfect for hunting, fishing, cycling, camping, canoeing, boating, hiking and simply connecting with the outdoors. This sort of outdoorsman's paradise should be celebrated, and that's exactly what they do, year after year.

The weekend kicks off with a golf tournament and a wildlife exhibit, set to the background of live music. The fun continues on Saturday with an archery contest, bass tournament, cutest camo contest and more live music. Come hungry, the aroma from the various food vendors will tempt the taste buds, and there's more…. Chainsaw art, arts and crafts vendors, and fishing and hunting gear will keep festival goers browsing all afternoon. Meanwhile, there are courses available to educate on how to be a responsible outdoorsman. Antler scoring seminars, boating and water safety tips, hunting safety, and weapons registration are just a few of the educational opportunities available.

Check the Poteau Main Street website or give them a call for more information.

Jalapeño Dip

1½ pounds cream cheese, softened
1 (9-ounce) jar sweet pickle relish
2 tablespoons Worcestershire sauce
½ teaspoon garlic powder
1 tablespoon grated onion
6 jalapeños, 3-inches long, cored, seeded and coarsely
  chopped

Combine all ingredients; mix well. Chill in refrigerator at least 2 hours. Serve with Cracked Black Pepper Triscuits for a hot and sweet hors d'oeuvre.

from Tom's lovely Mother, June
Redbud Ridge Vineyard & Winery

Redbud Ridge Vineyard & Winery

7301 East Highway 9 • Norman
405-321-9463 • www.redbudridgewinery.com

The winery is tucked into the cross timber forest of Oklahoma. Nature loving and natural Oklahoma wines are companions on this site just east of Norman, on Highway 9. They specialize in wines that pair well with food. From the intense, bold flavor of the "Big Red Steak Wine" to the complex lightness of the "3 Roses" wine you can be sure that you can find an appropriate wine for dinner. When chilled the Alsatian style Riesling or the "3 Roses" works well as cocktail wines.

Cowboy Caviar

1 can black beans, rinsed and drained
2 cans chopped black olives
2 tablespoons oil
2 tablespoons lime juice
¼ teaspoon ground cumin
¼ teaspoon salt
¼ teaspoon crushed red pepper
1 (8-ounce) package of cream cheese, softened

Combine beans, olives, oil, lime juice and spices. Let sit 2 hours. Spread cream cheese on a plate and top with bean mixture. Refrigerate until ready to serve.

Historic Stockyards City
"Centennial Cookbook" (2010)

Hot Mustard

1 cup mustard
1 cup apple cider vinegar
2 eggs, well beaten
1 cup sugar
1 pinch salt

Combine mustard and vinegar and soak overnight. Combine mustard mixture with remaining ingredients and cook in a double boiler until thick. Allow to cool slightly. Fill half pint jars with warm mustard and refrigerate. Must be kept in the refrigerator. Too much on a warm ham sandwich will water the eyes and drain the sinuses. I always double this recipe because it can be used on so many things including as a gift.

from Tom's lovely Mother, June
Redbud Ridge Vineyard & Winery

Caramel Fruit Dip

1 (8-ounce) package cream cheese, softened
½ cup brown sugar
2 teaspoons vanilla

Stir all ingredients together. Serve with apples, grapes and other favorite fruits.

Jane Apple
Hitching Post Bed & Breakfast

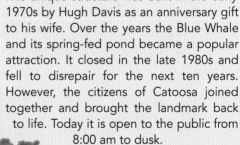

The Blue Whale of Catoosa

An iconic stop along old Route 66 is the Blue Whale of Catoosa. This unique structure was built in the early 1970s by Hugh Davis as an anniversary gift to his wife. Over the years the Blue Whale and its spring-fed pond became a popular attraction. It closed in the late 1980s and fell to disrepair for the next ten years. However, the citizens of Catoosa joined together and brought the landmark back to life. Today it is open to the public from 8:00 am to dusk.

Sweet and Spicy Watermelon Salsa

¼ cup lime juice
3 tablespoons brown sugar
3 cups chopped Southeast
  Oklahoma watermelon
½ cup minced red onion
2 tablespoons chopped mint
  leaves

½ teaspoon grated whole nutmeg
2 tablespoons minced, seeded
  jalapeño pepper
⅓ cup fresh cilantro
1 cucumber, peeled and chopped
Salt to taste

Whisk lime juice (fresh squeezed best) and sugar until sugar is dissolved. Combine with remaining ingredients in medium-size bowl. Toss gently. Refrigerate overnight. Use only mint leaves and not the stems.

Janie Oney
Official Salsa of the Valliant Watermelon Festival

Valliant Watermelon Festival

Last Weekend of July

Terry Hunt Building • Valliant City Park
580-933-5050 • www.valliantchamber.org

The annual Valliant Watermelon Festival is held on the last weekend in July. The festival kicks off with a parade through downtown Valliant on Friday evening, leading everyone to the City Park for a free gospel concert. Saturday events include a USATF sanctioned 5K run, youth fun run, car show, turtle races, the Country Showdown Talent Search contest, quilt show, dash-hound dog races, photography show, pony rides, watermelon eating and seed-spitting contest, horseshoe tournament, Big Melon Weigh-off and auction, watermelon toss, street dance, and many more activities and events. The Chamber of Commerce hosts a pancake breakfast, complete with many watermelon items. Later in the day the Chamber also gives out free watermelon slices. But the watermelon goodies don't end there. Watermelon slushies, watermelon parfaits and the famous watermelon salsa are on hand for the taking.

Black Bean Salsa

1 can black beans, rinsed and drained
1 (8-ounce) can shoepeg corn
1 (14.5-ounce) can diced tomatoes
1 (10-ounce) can diced tomatoes with green chiles
8 ounces Italian dressing
1 medium onion, chopped
1 medium jalapeño, chopped (optional)

Mix all ingredients together and refrigerate 3 hours. Serve with tortilla chips.

Turner Falls Park

Turner Falls Park

I-35 and Highway 77 • Davis
580-369-2988 • www.turnerfallspark.com

Located in Davis is Turner Falls Park, an adventurous and family-friendly destination nestled below the famous Arbuckle Mountains. Hiking trails, natural swimming areas, a 77-foot waterfall, caves, and sandy beaches are just a few of the natural wonders waiting to be discovered. After swimming and hiking, a tour of the Rock Castle is a must!

This 1500-acre area has been entertaining guests since the mid-1800s and continues to provide endless entertainment and education for locals, tourist and students, year after year.

There are cabins, rv hookups, picnic sites, bath houses and a number of concessions and gift shops on the premises.

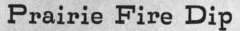

Prairie Fire Dip

1 tablespoon finely chopped onion
1 (16-ounce) can refried beans
½ cup shredded provolone cheese
1 clove garlic, minced
2 to 3 teaspoons chili powder
Hot pepper sauce to taste
2 tablespoons butter (optional)
Large corn chips

In a saucepan, combine onion, beans, cheese, garlic, chili powder, hot pepper sauce and butter, if desired. Cook over low heat until cheese is melted and dip is thoroughly heated. Serve with corn chips.

Kim Burge
The Dehydrator

Jalapeño Pepper Poppers

4 ounces cream cheese, softened
¼ cup shredded Cheddar cheese
8 jalapeños (about 2 inches long sliced in half lengthwise)
16 slices bacon, cooked
1 (8-ounce) can crescent dinner rolls

Preheat oven to 375°. In bowl, mix cream cheese and Cheddar cheese together. Fill sliced jalapeño with cheese mixture. Wrap each filled pepper with slice of bacon. Roll out crescent dough and separate into triangles. Slice each crescent in half lengthwise. Put bacon-wrapped pepper on dough and roll up dough around pepper, fully covering. Place each rolled pepper on ungreased cookie sheet. Bake until golden brown.

Clint Eaves
Chisholm Trail Historical Preservation Society, Inc.

Golden-Raisin Pecan Cheese Log

1 teaspoon ground mustard
1 teaspoon warm water
2 (8-ounce) packages cream cheese, softened
¼ cup real mayonnaise
¼ teaspoon ground nutmeg
2 cups shredded Colby cheese
1 cup golden raisins (may substitute dried cranberries)
1 cup chopped pecans, divided

Dissolve mustard in warm water. In a separate bowl, cream together cream cheese, mayonnaise and nutmeg. Add cheese, raisins, mustard mixture and ½ cup pecans. Divide in half, roll each into log shape. Wrap in clear wrap and refrigerate 2 hours. Roll log again while still in the wrap to make a smooth log. On clean wrap, sprinkle remaining nuts, roll log till coated, refrigerate. Serve with Wheat Thins or Triscuits.

Buffalo Creek Guest Ranch

Whistle Stop Bistro

Known for their delicious chicken salad sandwiches, paninis, soups and desserts, the Whistle Stop Bistro has a light and fun atmosphere suitable for the whole family. Located at 2700 North Main Street in McAlester, it is open Monday through Friday for lunch. Check out their Facebook page or give them a call at 918-423-8620.

Chip off the Old Block Miller Family Nachos

1 (16-ounce) bag corn chips, such as Doritos or Tostitos
1 (8-ounce) can refried beans
½ pound sliced Monterey Jack cheese
1 (6-ounce) jar pickled sliced jalapeño peppers, drained

Preheat oven to 300°. Scatter corn chips on a baking sheet. Spoon a portion of the refried beans onto each corn chip. Drape cheese slices over chips, and scatter jalapeño peppers over cheese. Bake 5 minutes, or until cheese has melted and nachos are hot. Enjoy!

Roger Miller Music & Arts Festival

Do-Wacka-Do Trail Run

The Roger Miller Museum sponsors the Do-Wacka-Do Trail Run south of Erick each year in September. It is a scenic, but challenging, trail. For information on the trail run call 580-515-1540.

Roger Miller Music & Arts Festival

Fourth Saturday in October

Roger Miller Museum • Erick
Corner of Roger Miller Boulevard and Sheb Wooley Avenue
580-526-3833 • www.rogermillermuseum.com

The Roger Miller Festival is held every year in Erick, Oklahoma, on the fourth Saturday in October. Erick is the home town of Roger Miller. He not only was a unique singer/songwriter/entertainer, but inspired the realization that no matter who you are, anything is possible.

The downtown stage boasts local talent as well as out of town performers. There are arts and crafts vendors, delicious food, the Do-Wacka-Do Crazy Hat Contest, pet costume contest and parade.

Don't miss the All-Wheels car show and poker run. Be sure to bring the kids; they will enjoy pony rides, wagon rides, and fun TV characters. Recent additions to the festival include a song writing and talent contest. At 7:00 on Saturday night the big concert starts, held each year in the Clifford Macklin Auditorium.

Dried Beef Log

1 (8-ounce) package cream
   cheese, softened
¼ cup Parmesan cheese
1 tablespoon horseradish
⅓ cup chopped green olives

1 tablespoon Worcestershire
   sauce
2 tablespoons milk
1 small glass jar dried beef

Mix all together and roll into a log or ball. Refrigerate until firm.
Serve with crackers.

Karolyn Anders
Holiday in the Park

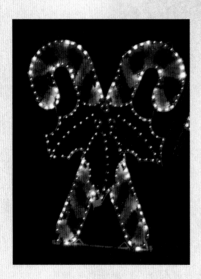

Holiday in the Park

Third Week in November through New Year's Day

Elmer Thomas Park • 3rd Street and Ferris • Lawton
580-351-4173 or 580-695-8988
www.cityof.lawton.ok.us • www.lawtonfortsillchamber.com

Christmas is a time of joy, a time for love and cheer, and a time for making memories to last throughout the year. The Holiday in the Park Parade and Tree Lighting is always the Saturday BEFORE Thanksgiving and runs through New Years Day. Without the generous support of the many businesses and citizen's in the community, the Holiday season would not be as bright, merry and cheerful. There are Holiday displays scattered throughout the Park and may be viewed with a drive through the Park or walking. Elmer Thomas Park, the site of the event is easily accessible from I-44 going north or south. Seasonal events are planned throughout the year and they are sponsored by Holiday in the Park. Check out their Facebook page under "Lawtons Holiday in the Park". The Museum of the Great Plains is adjacent to the Park for further enjoyment.

Chicken Hotties

6 boneless chicken thighs
3 jalapeño peppers, seeded and cut each into 8 matchsticks
12 slices bacon, cut in half
Salt and pepper
Barbecue sauce

Cut thighs into 4 equal pieces, lay 1 jalapeño matchstick on each and wrap in bacon. Secure with toothpicks. Salt and pepper to taste. Grill over medium heat until bacon is crisp and chicken is cooked through, about 12 minutes. Brush with sauce and serve. Makes 24.

Oklahoma Championship Steak Cook-Off

Crab Roll-Ups

1 (10-ounce) package frozen chopped spinach, thawed and squeezed dry
1 envelope vegetable soup mix
½ cup mayonnaise
½ cup sour cream
¼ cup chutney
1 (18-ounce) package imitation crabmeat, chopped
1 (8-ounce) package cream cheese, softened
⅛ teaspoon garlic powder
⅛ teaspoon onion powder
12 (8-inch) flour tortillas

Combine spinach, soup mix, mayonnaise and sour cream; mix well and refrigerate 1 hour. In a separate bowl, combine chutney, crabmeat, cream cheese, garlic powder and onion powder. Refrigerate 1 hour. Spread first mixture evenly over 6 tortillas and second mixture evenly over remaining 6 tortillas. Place them together, roll into tight rolls, and refrigerate 30 minutes. Cut into 1-inch rounds. Yields approximately 3 dozen.

Mary Andrews
The Dehydrator

Party Sandwiches

SANDWICHES:

2 packages Hawaiian rolls

1 pound honey ham

½ pound baby Swiss cheese

½ pound provolone cheese

Cut rolls in half so you have tops and bottoms. Cover 9x13-inch pan with roll bottoms. Layer ham and cheeses on rolls. Then put tops of the rolls on.

DRESSING:

2 sticks butter

4 tablespoons sugar

4 tablespoons honey mustard

2 tablespoons poppy seeds

2 tablespoons dried onion flakes

Melt dressing ingredients together. Pour hot dressing over top of rolls. Cut between rolls so dressing can spread between them. Bake uncovered at 400° for 13 to 15 minutes.

Watonga Cheese Festival

Interesting History...

Watonga was the childhood home of Clarence Nash, the voice of Donald Duck. Also, The Ferguson Museum, home of Oklahoma's sixth Territorial Governor, is found in Watonga.

Winter's Day au Lait

2 cups hot brewed coffee
2 cups milk, heated
¾ cup liquid coffee creamer
   (holiday flavors like pumpkin or
   peppermint add a special touch)

1 tablespoon pure vanilla extract
   (not imitation)
¾ teaspoon ground cinnamon
¾ teaspoon ground nutmeg
Cinnamon sticks (optional)

Combine all ingredients (except cinnamon sticks) in a large container. Pour into mugs and serve with cinnamon sticks.

Talihina Fall Foliage Festival

Talihina Fall Foliage Festival

Last Weekend in October

Talihina School
Highway 271 North • Talihina
918-567-3434 • www.talihinacc.com

When traveling through the southeast part of the state in October, be sure to visit the Talihina Fall Foliage Festival. This fun event has something for all interests—arts and craft vendors, delicious food, a 1967-1969 Camaro parade, car show, 5K run, children's activities and the Choctaw Indian Cultural and Heritage Area. Legends of the Mountains Story Telling is certain to capture the imaginations of all who attend. Admission is free.

Apricot Spice Tea

½ cup Tang

4 small boxes apricot
  jello

1 cup lemonade mix

½ cup instant tea

1 cup sugar

Mix all together and store in an airtight container. Add 3 teaspoons to 1 cup hot water and enjoy.

Jane Apple
Hitching Post Bed & Breakfast

Bigfoot in Oklahoma

Cryptid: Any creature that may or may not exist.

And so goes the legend of Bigfoot. For centuries, reports of the large, ape-like cryptid have covered the globe. Scientists do not acknowledge Bigfoot's existence and consider it the stuff of folklore. However, thousands of eye-witnesses believe differently, and many of those sightings happen in Oklahoma. Almost 100 sightings happen each year throughout the state, drawing field investigators and Bigfoot enthusiasts from all over the world. So the next time you're out on the trail, camping by the lake, or taking an afternoon hike, be sure to bring your camera to document a Bigfoot sighting of your own.

Raspberry Punch

48 ounces lemon-lime soda
1 quart raspberry juice
1 can frozen lemonade
1 quart raspberry sherbet

Combine soda, raspberry juice and lemonade in a large punch bowl. Add raspberry sherbet and serve.

Karolyn Anders
Holiday in the Park

Fruity Punch

2 packages Kool-Aid, any flavor
1 to 2 cups sugar
1 (6-ounce) can frozen lemonade
   concentrate
½ can pineapple juice

1 bottle 7-Up or Sprite
Lemon or lime slices, optional
Frozen sliced sweetened
   strawberries, optional
Lemon juice, optional

Mix together everything but the 7-Up and fruit. Add enough water to fill a 1 gallon jar or pitcher and chill. Pour some punch in a mold and freeze for ice ring. When punch is chilled, pour half of the punch into a punch bowl with ice ring and add remaining 7-Up. Add slices of fruit if desired and about half a container of strawberries if using strawberry or cherry Kool-Aid. Add some lemon juice if it is not tart enough.

Any flavor Kool-Aid can be used depending on color scheme or flavor desired. Orange Kool-Aid is also good using orange juice concentrate in place of the lemonade and is very pretty with orange slices. Lemon or lime Kool-Aid are good with either the lemonade or limeade concentrates.

Sondra Martin
Bedstead Retreat

Lemonade

12 lemons
1½ cups sugar
3 bottles Apollinaris sparkling water

Squeeze lemons and sweeten. Add Apollinaris water when ready to serve (not before).

Mrs. Overholser, circa 1903
Overholser Mansion

Overholser Mansion

Open to the public Tues – Sat 10:00 am to 3:00 pm

405 NW 15th Street • Oklahoma City
405-525-5325 • www.overholsermansion.org

Built in 1903 on what was then the outskirts of Oklahoma City, this landmark is the most visible legacy of Henry Overholser, the man known as the Father of Oklahoma City. As Oklahoma City blossomed at the turn of the century, and the elegant neighborhood of Heritage Hills developed around the Overholsers' home, this late-Victorian mansion served as Oklahoma City's showplace and social center.

The Overholser Mansion is listed on the National Register of Historic Places, and is located within Oklahoma City's oldest historic district. This three-story chateau-esque home is replete with original furnishings, one-of-a-kind works of art, hand-painted canvas walls, and lavish fixtures. The Overholsers retained the first floor's original 1903 charm, while the second floor reflects the family's changing tastes through the decades.

Managed by Preservation Oklahoma on behalf of the Oklahoma Historical Society, the Mansion is undergoing restoration. Visitors can learn about the efforts to preserve this landmark as they tour the Mansion.

The Overholser Mansion is conveniently located five minutes from downtown Oklahoma City and offers visitors a look into the economic, architectural, and social history of Oklahoma City and the Overholser family.

"White Lightnin'" Milkshakes

Merle Haggard wrote that "white lightnin's still the biggest thrill of all in Muskogee, Oklahoma, USA" in his 1969 hit song. It's still a thrill, but we serve ours with a cherry on top!

4 cups vanilla ice cream
2 teaspoons vanilla extract
⅓ cup sugar
2 cups milk, less for thicker milkshakes
Whipped cream
Chopped pecans
Maraschino cherries

Using a blender or milkshake machine, blend ice cream, extract, sugar and milk together until smooth. Serve in tall glasses with a straw. Top with whipped cream, chopped pecans and a cherry.

Heritage Days: A Living History Festival

Soups, Salads & Breads

Cold Peach Soup

5 large, fully ripe peaches, peeled and quartered
¼ cup sugar (more if needed)
1 cup sour cream
¼ cup fresh lemon juice
¼ cup sherry or white wine
1 tablespoon orange juice concentrate
Peeled and sliced fresh peaches for garnish

Purée peaches and sugar in blender. Mix in sour cream. Add lemon juice, sherry or wine and orange juice; blend until smooth. Refrigerate until well chilled. Serves 6 to 8.

Mary A Fitzhugh
Chisholm Trail Historical Preservation Society, Inc.

Strawberry Soup

15 ounces frozen strawberries, thawed (with juice)
15 ounces sour cream
½ ounce (1 tablespoon) grenadine syrup
1 ounce (2 tablespoons) vanilla extract
3 ounces (scant ½ cup) sifted powdered sugar (measure after sifting)
2 ounces (¼ cup) half & half

Mix strawberries and sour cream. Beat slowly until well mixed. Add grenadine, vanilla and sugar, mixing constantly, until smooth consistency. Add half & half last, mixing only until well blended. Chill. Stir well before serving. Serves 6.

Mary A Fitzhugh
Chisholm Trail Historical Preservation Society, Inc.

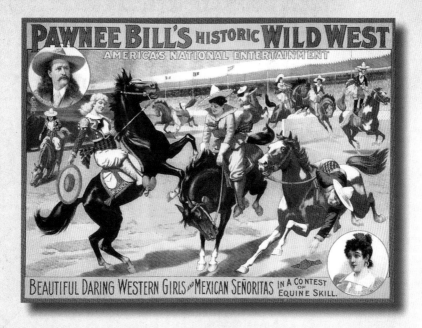

Wild West Kickin' Cheese Soup

1 can cream of potato soup
1 can Veg-All
1 can yellow hominy
½ can Rotel (or more if you like it hotter)
½ pound Velveeta cheese, chunks

Put soup, vegetables and tomatoes in a crockpot and cook on low 4 hours. Add Velveeta in the last hour. Enjoy!

Pawnee Bill Museum and Original Wild West Show

Potato Soup

1½ pounds potatoes, peeled
   and diced
¼ cup butter
½ cup chopped onion
3 cups chicken broth
Salt and pepper to taste
¼ cup all-purpose flour
1½ cups milk
6 cloves garlic, crushed
¼ teaspoon rosemary
¼ teaspoon basil
¼ teaspoon thyme
¼ teaspoon tarragon
Chopped fresh parsley,
   for garnish

In a large pot, sauté potatoes in butter with onion until onion is translucent.
Add chicken broth, salt and pepper; cook until potatoes are tender. In a
separate bowl, mix flour and milk. When well blended, add to potato soup
mixture. Add garlic, rosemary, basil, thyme and tarragon and boil 15 to 20
minutes. Garnish individual servings with parsley.

Choctaw Land Run Festival

Choctaw Land Run Festival
April

Choctaw Creek Park • Choctaw
405-390-8198 • www.choctawfestival.org

Come celebrate the Oklahoma Land Run of April 22, 1889. This was a historical event in which land was open for the taking to whoever arrived first. The east boundary of the 1889 run was the Indian Meridian. Today it is known as Indian Meridian Road and it runs right through Choctaw.

The weekend is filled with historical presentations, re-enactor encampments, historical figure presentations, cowboy encampments, cavalry encampments, jailhouse, gun fights, old-fashioned games, and food vendors to suit all taste. Admission and parking is free of charge, making this living museum a must-see for travelers and history buffs alike.

Oklahoma Land Run Monument

"Flashy" Baked Potato Soup

⅔ cup butter
⅔ cup flour
7 cups milk
4 large potatoes, baked, cooled, peeled and cubed
½ medium onion, chopped
12 slices bacon, fried and crumbled
1¼ cups grated sharp Cheddar cheese
¾ teaspoon salt
½ teaspoon pepper
1 heaping tablespoon chicken base

In large Dutch oven, melt butter. Stir in flour, heat and stir until smooth. Gradually add milk, stirring constantly, until thickened. Add potatoes and onions. Bring to boil, stirring constantly. Reduce heat and simmer 10 minutes. Add remaining ingredients and stir until cheese is melted. If too thick, add more milk.

Courtesy of Santa's Old Broads
Pelican Festival

Nacho Cheese Soup

1 cup grated carrot
1 cup finely chopped celery
1 cup chopped onions
3 cans chicken broth
1 can cream of chicken soup
1 can Rotel (diced tomatoes and chiles)
1 cup grated sharp Cheddar cheese
1 pound American Processed cheese, cubed
1 tablespoon garlic powder
Salt and pepper to taste

Cook vegetables in broth until tender. Add rest of the ingredients and heat until cheese melts. Serve with corn chips.

Watonga Cheese Festival

Cheese Soup

3 cups diced carrots
3 cups diced celery
3 cups diced onions
1½ cups butter
9 tablespoons cornstarch

1½ cups flour
6 cans instant milk
6 cans chicken broth
6 cups grated cheese
6 pounds Velveeta cheese, diced

Sauté vegetables in butter. Add cornstarch and flour. Mix instant milk according to package directions. In a big pot, combine chicken broth and milk, adding milk about 2 cups at a time, heating slowly. Add veggies to broth and bring to a boil. Reduce heat, add cheese and stir until melted.

Noble House Bed & Breakfast and Restaurant

Ham and Hominy Chowder

1 tablespoon vegetable oil
1 pound red potatoes, washed
1 medium onion, chopped
1 medium green or red bell pepper, chopped
1¼ cups chopped cooked ham

½ cup chopped celery
1 can hominy, undrained
1 tablespoon flour
1½ teaspoons thyme leaves
1½ teaspoons salt and pepper
1½ cups milk

In 3-quart saucepan, combine oil, potatoes, onion, pepper, ham and celery; cook 10 minutes, over low heat, stirring occasionally. Gradually add hominy, flour, thyme, salt and pepper, stirring constantly. Add milk and bring to a boil. Reduce heat. Simmer, covered, 30 minutes or until potatoes are tender.

LaVonne Terry
The Dehydrator

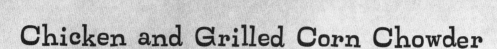

Chicken and Grilled Corn Chowder

⅛ cup olive oil

1 small green Anaheim chiles, seeded and diced

½ medium red onion, chopped

⅔ cup chopped celery

⅔ cup diced carrot

⅔ cup diced red bell pepper

1 small jalapeño, seeded and diced

6 ears corn, grilled and kernels cut from cob, use at least 3-inch cob

1 pound cooked chicken, diced

1 gallon chicken broth

1 pint heavy cream

1 tablespoon minced thyme

1 garlic clove, chopped

1 bay leaf

Salt and pepper to taste

Pinch cayenne pepper

2 teaspoons cornstarch

¼ cup water

In a large kettle, heat olive oil and sauté green chile peppers, red onion, celery, carrots, red bell pepper, jalapeño and grilled corn kernels (cut from cob) 5 minutes. Add chicken, chicken broth, cream, thyme, garlic, bay leaf, salt, pepper and cayenne pepper. Dissolve cornstarch in water and stir into soup. Simmer gently 30 minutes.

Chef Neil Lindenbaum
Paul's Place Steakhouse

PAUL'S PLACE

Paul's Place Steakhouse and Billy Boy BBQ

120 West MacArthur • Shawnee
www.paulsplacesteakhouse.com
405-275-5650 Paul's Place Steakhouse
405-275-2040 Billy Boy BBQ

Billy Boy Barbeque is a family owned and operated establishment. The Scott family bought it in 1973 and as its customer base has grown, so has the restaurant. Billy Boy's has a hometown appeal, and customers feel comfortable as soon as they walk in the door. Serving some of the best barbeque in town, Billy Boy's charm and good service bring diners back again and again.

Paul's Place Steakhouse was also opened by the Scott family. They felt the area could use something a little more upscale than barbeque and believed just about everybody likes a good steak. The restaurant has now been open for several years, and it is THE place to celebrate a special occasion or to just have a great meal. In addition to steak, the menu also includes salads, pasta and seafood. A full bar is also available. Both restaurants offer catering and the full menu is available for take out.

Great Cajun Gumbo

Time consuming but well worth it!!!

2 cups cooking oil
2 cups flour
2 tablespoons gumbo filé
2 large onions, diced
1 large bell pepper, diced
4 cloves garlic, crushed
3 stalks celery, diced
1 whole chicken, cut up into separate pieces
Approximately 1 gallon hot boiling water or broth
3 cups sliced southern smoked sausage
2 bunches green onions, fully sliced
3 tablespoons Tony Chachere Creole seasoning, or to taste
Salt and pepper to taste

Heat oil and brown flour and gumbo filé in large pot over medium heat, stirring constantly until roux gets to a dark chocolate color. Add onions, bell peppers, garlic and celery and stir a little. Add chicken gradually, stirring constantly, and begin adding hot water or broth at this point (be careful not to let steam burn you). Continue stirring until fully mixed. Add sausage, bring to a boil, reduce heat, cover and let simmer as long as possible. Add green onions, then seasonings to taste. Serve with rice, cornbread and pepper sauce.

Clint Eaves
Chisholm Trail Historical Preservation Society, Inc.

Chili for a Crowd

10 pounds ground beef
1 (industrial-size) can pinto beans, drained
3 big ladles jalapeños
2 big ladles jalapeño juice
6 tablespoons chili powder
7 tablespoons cumin
2 (industrial-size) cans tomato sauce

Brown meat in a large pot; drain. Add all other ingredients and simmer 2 hours.

Heartland Cruise Car Show

High Plains Taco Soup

1 pound ground beef
1 small onion, chopped
1 can chopped green chilies
1 cup water
1 can whole kernel corn, drained
1 can kidney beans
1 can stewed tomatoes
1 can Rotel tomatoes
1 package mild taco seasoning
1 package ranch dressing mix
Tortilla chips
Shredded Cheddar cheese
Sour cream

In a large pot, brown ground beef with onion and green chilies; drain off fat. Add water, corn, beans, tomatoes, taco seasoning and ranch dressing mix. Bring to a boil, stirring frequently. Cover and reduce heat. Allow to simmer 20 minutes. Serve on top of tortilla chips, top with Cheddar cheese and sour cream.

Will Rogers' Favorite Recipe

Will Rogers always said his favorite dish was beans and that's what he always asked for when he came home to visit—beans, any style, any kind, and cornbread. But "I sure do love my chili," he wrote on July 17, 1927, as republished in James M. Smallwood and Steven K. Gragert, eds, Will Rogers' Weekly Articles:Volume 3: The Coolidge Years, 1927-1929 (Stillwater: Oklahoma State University Press, 1981) 47. Will Rogers Jr. in a 1954 letter to Mrs. E.V. Jordan, 1623 Louden Heights Rd., Charleston, W.V., wrote that he had found his Aunt Theda's (Betty Rogers' sister) chili recipe his dad particularly liked:

1 pound ground round steak	1 can tomatoes
1 onion, chopped	1 can (small) pimento, chopped
Salt to taste	2 cans red kidney beans

Sauté round steak and onion with salt in a skillet, cooking until steak is slightly brown. Add tomatoes and pimentos, cooking about 2 minutes. Cover with hot water and cook over low heat about 1 hour, then add kidney beans. Continue cooking 30 to 45 minutes.

Will Rogers & Wiley Post Fly-In

Will Rogers Museum and Will Rogers Days

Will Rogers Days mark Will's birth on November 4, 1879, and the November 4, 1938, opening of the Will Rogers Memorial Museum in Claremore. Traditional events are a birthday party at the Will Rogers Birthplace Ranch, trick roping, children's musical, Family Night at the Museum, Pocahontas Indian Women's Club Tribute at the Memorial Museum, and Saturday parade down Will Rogers Boulevard through the town of Claremore. Special guests are family members and people from Will Rogers' past.

Will Rogers & Wiley Post Fly-In

The Sunday nearest August 15th

Will Rogers Birthplace Ranch • Oologah
800-324-9455

This is an annual event on the Sunday nearest August 15, celebrating the lives of Will Rogers and pilot Wiley Post. Pilots land new and antique aircraft on a 2,000-foot grass strip adjacent to the house in which Will Rogers was born. The Fly-In marks the anniversary of the August 15, 1935 crash that claimed the lives of Will Rogers and Wiley Post in an Alaskan plane crash. Children's activities, Cherokee story telling, antique and classic car show, music, food vendors and tours of the home in which Will was born are all included.

Chili of Champions

1 pound ground beef
2 small onions, chopped
½ cup chopped green pepper
1 teaspoon minced garlic
2 (16-ounce) cans kidney beans,
  rinsed and drained
2 (14-ounce) cans stewed tomatoes
1 (28-ounce) can crushed tomatoes
1 (6-ounce) can tomato paste

1 (12-ounce) bottle beer
  (non-alcoholic may be used)
¼ cup chili powder
¾ teaspoon dried oregano
¾ teaspoon hot pepper sauce
¼ teaspoon sugar
¼ teaspoon salt
¼ teaspoon black pepper

Cook ground beef, onions and peppers in a large saucepan over medium heat. When beef is browned, add garlic and cook an additional 1 to 2 minutes. Drain. Return to heat, adding remaining ingredients and bringing to a boil. Reduce heat and simmer, uncovered, an additional 10 to 12 minutes. Yields 12 to 14 servings.

Santa Fe Depot & Museum
Shawnee Convention & Visitors Bureau

Santa Fe Depot Museum

Oklahoma Style Chili

2 pounds stew meat
1 pound ground beef
¼ cup vegetable oil
2 garlic cloves, minced
2 cups water
2 teaspoons cumin
2 green bell peppers, chopped and seeded
2 onions, chopped
12 ounces canned tomato paste

56 ounces canned chopped tomatoes
1 tablespoon sugar
1 tablespoon salt
1 tablespoon crushed red pepper flakes
½ tablespoon black pepper
¼ pound grated sharp Cheddar cheese

In a crockpot, brown meat in oil. Add remaining ingredients (except cheese) and simmer 2 hours. Serve in bowls and cover with grated cheese. Serves 4.

J.M. Davis Arms & Historical Museum

Three Rivers Museum

Located in the historic Midland Valley Depot in downtown Muskogee is the Three Rivers Museum. The museum was established in 1989 to preserve the settlement story and history of the Three Rivers Region of Oklahoma. In addition to many permanent exhibits, the museum hosts themed events and historic tours throughout the year. While you're there, stop by the gift shop and pick up your very own "Okie from Muskogee" t-shirt!

Cowboy Stew

1 pound ground beef
1 small onion, chopped
1 small green bell pepper,
   chopped
½ teaspoon minced garlic, optional
1 (15-ounce) can whole kernel corn,
   do not drain

1 (15-ounce) can diced tomatoes,
   do not drain
1 (15-ounce) can ranch style beans,
   do not drain
1 teaspoon chili powder or to taste
½ teaspoon salt

Brown meat with onion, bell pepper and garlic; do not drain. Add remaining ingredients (do not drain cans). Simmer 20 minutes or longer.

McAlester Wild West Festival

McAlester Wild West Festival

First Weekend in October

McAlester
918-329-9417
www.facebook.com/McAlestersOldTownFestival

Old Town Association and Main Street McAlester present the McAlester Wild West Festival each year in Historic Old Town McAlester—where McAlester began. McAlester Wild West Festival features Wild West Gun Fights, live country music, trick roping, a 5K run, street dance, poker run, street performers, games, and lots of other fun events. There will be a great variety of food as well as lots of antique shopping, free museum tour, fun rides, historic tours and games. This fun festival offers something for everyone. When you get there, be sure to get your Sheriff Badge for a chance to win a door prize.

Rose-Bud Salad

1 package coleslaw mix
1 bunch green onions, chopped
1 can water chestnuts, drained and chopped
1 package almonds
1 package sunflower seeds
2 packages beef ramen noodles, uncooked and broken
   (Reserve the seasoning)

Mix all the ingredients, except ramen seasoning, together.

DRESSING:

½ cup sugar
⅓ cup oil
⅓ cup vinegar
1 package ramen noodles beef seasoning

Mix together and heat in saucepan over low-medium heat.
Pour over vegetable mixture and toss.

Southern Belle Restaurant

Fun Fact

Heavener Runestone Park is a 55-acre park located near the city of Heavener, Oklahoma. Formerly a state park of Oklahoma, it is now owned and operated by the city of Heavener. A runestone is a large stone carved by Scandinavians in the late Viking Age.

Southern Belle Restaurant

821 Highway 59 North • Heavener
918-653-4458
www.facebook.com/southernbelleheavener

An authentic train car... Oklahoma's best fried chicken strips... Homemade candy cheesecakes... This is the experience of the Southern Belle Restaurant. The Southern Belle is a 1905 model train car that has been restored to a lovely little restaurant with the most amazing and savory home cooking. The restaurant is most famous for its Southern Belle chicken. The chicken is marinated boneless strips which are breaded, fried, and served with their famous house dipping sauce. The menu has tasty steaks, shrimp, fish, burgers, sandwiches, and pork chops, all prepared in a down-home fashion. Of course, there is delicious homemade pie... The perfect ending to a perfect meal.

The Southern Belle Restaurant is one dining experience you will not want to miss!

Spinach Salad

1 bag fresh spinach leaves
1 apple, sliced
2 chopped green onions
Crisp fried bacon bits
½ package slivered toasted almonds
½ package dried cranberries
Grated Parmesan cheese

Combine all ingredients in a large salad bowl.

DRESSING:

1½ cups sugar
2 teaspoons dry mustard
¾ cup cider vinegar (or use part cider vinegar and
    part raspberry vinegar)
2 cups olive or canola oil
2 tablespoons poppy seeds (optional)

In a separate bowl, combine sugar, dry mustard and
vinegar, whisking briskly. Continuing to whisk, add oil
slowly. Add poppy seeds last. Pour desired amount over
salad and toss.

Kim Burge
The Dehydrator

Cucumber Salad

3 to 4 medium-size cucumbers
1 teaspoon salt
½ cup cream

2 teaspoons sugar
2 teaspoons vinegar
Black pepper

Peel cucumbers then slice or grate (according to your preference). Salt cucumbers and refrigerate. When ready to serve, drain cucumbers. Mix cream, sugar and vinegar. Pour over cucumbers and sprinkle with black pepper to taste.

Kolache Festival

Gotebo Salad

1 cup sugar
½ cup vinegar
2 cans black-eyed peas, drained
   and rinsed

1 cup chopped green bell pepper
1 cup chopped onion
1 cup chopped celery

Cook sugar and vinegar until sugar dissolves. Pour over peas, green pepper, onion and celery; toss. Refrigerate overnight before serving.

Cathy Clement
Chisholm Trail Historical Preservation Society, Inc.

Fresh Mushroom Salad

1 pound fresh mushrooms
Fresh green onions to taste, chopped
Fresh parsley to taste, chopped
8 ounces mozzarella cheese

¼ cup vinegar
½ cup vegetable oil
3 teaspoons Cavender's Greek
Seasoning

Wash and slice mushrooms; mix with onion and parsley. Grate mozzarella cheese into a separate dish. Blend vinegar, vegetable oil and seasoning in a food processor or blender and place in a separate bowl. Immediately before serving, combine mushroom mixture with mozzarella cheese and dressing. Toss thoroughly. Serves 8.

Marge Jurgensmeyer
Miami Convention & Visitors Bureau

Events in Miami

Rich with Native American history and home to the longest stretch of the original Route 66 Ribbon Road, Miami is a city every traveler should aim to visit. Pronounced 'my-AM-uh,' this colorful city in the Northeastern corner of the state has celebrations throughout the year. Here is a sampling of just a few…

Rodeo Miami
May • Miami Fairgrounds

Oklahoma 8-Man All-Star Football Game at NEO
June • A&M College

Miami Route 66 Revvin' It Up Car Show & Cruise Night
June

Miami PBR
July

Ottawa County Free Fair
August

Miami NOW (Native Oklahoma Weekend)
October

Miami's Coleman Theatre

City of Miami

Miami Convention & Visitors Bureau
101 North Main Street
918-542-4435
www.visitmiamiok.com

There are plenty of places to rest
while traveling through Miami.

Hampton Inn & Suites
918.541.1500

Holiday Inn Express
918.542.7424

America's Best Value Inn
918.542.6681

Microtel Inn & Suites
918.540.3333

Legacy Inns & Suites

Deluxe Inn Motel
918.542.5600

Econolodge
918.542.6631

This three mile pavement is one of two sections of the original nine-foot wide road that remains intact. "Ribbon Road" continues to maintain a high degree of integrity because of the width of the road, the original setting, the original material which remains visible through gravel and eroded overlays of asphalt. The road conveys the feeling of its past environment. It is listed as an Oklahoma National Historic Landmark.

Cabbage Slaw

¼ cup mayonnaise
2 tablespoons milk
2 tablespoons vinegar
2 tablespoons sugar
1 teaspoon salt

Dash pepper
½ head cabbage, shredded
½ cup raisins (optional)
½ cup pineapple (optional)

Beat mayonnaise and milk with a fork until smooth. Add vinegar, sugar, salt and pepper and continue beating. Pour over shredded cabbage and stir to moisten. Add raisins or pineapple, if desired.

Jane Apple
Hitching Post Bed & Breakfast

Cabbage Salad

1 medium-size head cabbage, shredded
2 or 3 medium carrots, grated
1 cup raisins
½ cup mayonnaise
2 tablespoons sugar
1 teaspoon salt
1 tablespoon vinegar

Place shredded cabbage, grated carrots and raisins in bowl. Mix mayonnaise, sugar, salt and vinegar. Pour over cabbage and mix well.

Kolache Festival

Hot Potato Salad

5 to 6 potatoes
3 to 4 slices bacon, cubed
¼ cup sugar
1 tablespoon flour
½ cup vinegar

¼ cup water
1 egg, whole (not cooked)
¾ cup cubed celery
½ cup chopped onion
2 boiled eggs, sliced

Boil potatoes in skin until tender. Remove skins. Fry bacon. Mix sugar with flour and mix into fried bacon. At once add vinegar mixed with water. Bring to a boil; cool. Add 1 whole egg, bring to boil again and beat vigorously so that egg does not curdle. Pour over potatoes, celery, onions and sliced boiled eggs. Mix and serve warm.

Kolache Festival

Hot and Spicy Potato Salad

4 cups peeled and diced potatoes, cooked
3 boiled eggs, diced
⅓ cup finely chopped dill pickles
⅓ cup finely chopped sweet pickles
¼ cup finely chopped pimentos
¼ cup finely chopped pickled mild Golden Greek peppers
½ teaspoon finely chopped jalapeño peppers
¾ cup mayonnaise
1 pinch cayenne
Salt and pepper to taste
1 pinch garlic salt

Combine all ingredients and mix well. Chill 1 hour.

Elk City Fall Festival

Cherry Coke Salad

1 can sweet dark cherries
1 cup sugar
1 large package cherry Jell-O

½ cup boiling water
1 (8-ounce) can Coke
1 cup chopped nuts

Drain cherries reserving juice to a saucepan. Add sugar to cherry juice and bring to a boil. Add Jell-O and stir to dissolve. Add boiling water and Coke; cool. When mixture has cooled, add cherries and nuts. (Small apple pieces and halved grapes can also be added.) Pour into mold or dish. Chill in refrigerator until set.

Sharon Walker
Freedom Rodeo & Old Cowhand Reunion

Freedom Rodeo & Old Cowhand Reunion

Third Weekend in August

Freedom Rodeo Grounds
Freedom
580-621-3276
www.freedomrodeo.com

Nestled along the banks of the historic Cimarron River below towering gypsum bluffs, lies Oklahoma's smallest "Certified City", Freedom. From its earliest beginnings, this tiny town has gained a big reputation for its unique ability to persevere. Today, visitors to Freedom are astounded by the lingering presence of the "Old West", as nearly every building in the downtown area is fronted with native cedar wood in designs typical of an early day cow town.

Freedom is home to Alabaster Caverns State Park and the world's largest gypsum cave open to the public where guided tours are conducted through this underground wonderland of nature.

Freedom's population swells to about twenty-five times its normal size in August of each year as local residents and volunteers stage the annual "Freedom Rodeo and Old Cowhand Reunion". Recognized as one of Oklahoma's "Outstanding Events of the Year", this celebration features professional rodeo performances, live music and dancing, western arts and crafts, a free chuck-wagon feed, a reunion of cowhands near and far and the notorious melodramatic farce entitled "The Great Freedom Bank Robbery and Shoot-Out".

The cow town atmosphere, the beautiful surroundings and the genuine hospitality of its people all blend together to make Freedom a town as unique as the name itself.

Fresh Veggie Pasta Salad

1 large bag tri-color pasta swirls
1 large cucumber
3 medium yellow squash
2 medium zucchini squash
1 bunch fresh green onions
4 carrots
6 ribs celery
Salt and pepper to taste
1 bottle Hendrickson's Sweet
   Vinegar and Olive Oil salad
   dressing (may substitute with
   your favorite oil dressing)
Sugar to taste (optional)

Cook pasta per package directions. Slice cucumber, squash, onions and carrots in thin rounds and dice celery. Combine vegetables with pasta in a large bowl, adding salt and pepper to taste. Add salad dressing and sugar to taste. Toss thoroughly.

Janet Fitz
Woodward Main Street

Carrot-Macaroni Salad

1 (16-ounce) package curly noodles
3 large carrots, grated fine
¼ cup vinegar
2 cups real mayonnaise
½ onion, chopped fine
1 can sweetened condensed milk
1 green bell pepper, chopped
Salt and pepper to taste

Cook noodles. Mix remaining ingredients. Mix with noodles. Refrigerate overnight for best flavor.

Deborah Shady
Holiday in the Park

Mom's Chicken Salad

6 chicken breasts
3 boiled eggs, chopped
1 cup diced celery
1 can diced water chestnuts
1 cup diced onion
¾ cup chopped pecans

½ cup grated cheese
1½ cups Mom's Quick Sweet
    Pickles (see recipe below)
1 cup Miracle Whip
Salt and pepper to taste
⅓ cup sugar (optional)

Boil chicken till tender and dice into small chunks. Add next 8 ingredients, salt and pepper to taste, and mix thoroughly. Feel free to add more Miracle Whip for desired consistency. Sweeten with sugar if you like and mix well. Keep cool till served.

Merita Parsons
Woodward Main Street

Mom's Quick Sweet Pickles

1 gallon jar Vlasic whole dill pickles
6 cups sugar

In large bowl, cut pickles in rounds about ½-inch thick. Add sugar and mix. Let stand overnight with towel over bowl. Drain liquid, place pickles back in jar or sealed container. Store in refrigerator.

Merita Parsons
Woodward Main Street

Granny's Biscuits

Not too good for loosing weight, but they sure do taste good!

1 pinch baking soda
4 cups self-rising flour
¼ cup cold butter

2 cups old-fashioned buttermilk
¼ cup bacon grease

Preheat oven to 375°. In mixing bowl, combine baking soda into flour. Chop cold butter into flour mixture. Gently blend in buttermilk; do not over mix. Roll dough out to ⅝ inch thick. Cut into 3 inch rounds. Melt bacon grease in a warm a cast iron skillet. Roll rounds in bacon grease to cover top and bottom. Fill pan with rounds squeezed tightly together. Use a paper towel to soak up any excess grease. Bake approximately 20 minutes until golden brown.

Buffalo Creek Guest Ranch

Buffalo Creek Guest Ranch

6832 SE 235th Road • Talihina
877-527-4207 • www.BuffaloCreekGuestRanch.com

Have you ever longed to experience the days your grandparents talked about? It was a time when the grass was green and the air was fresh. Meals were gathered from the garden in the morning and prepared by hand for supper that night.

The stars weren't dimmed by city lights and you fell asleep with the windows open listening to the crickets, coyotes and hounds fussin' about who ruled the night. Wish no more as you can now experience all this in the luxurious comfort of Oklahoma's newest agritourism venture, the Buffalo Creek Guest Ranch.

Nestled in the mountains of beautiful southeast Oklahoma, the ranch offers a unique blend of a lodge-type outdoorsman adventure with an authentic ranch experience in a comfortable and cozy bed and breakfast environment. The Ranch is an all inclusive retreat designed to allow relaxation, fun and to let stress evaporate into the fresh mountain air.

Cornmeal Cheddar Biscuits

1½ cup all-purpose flour
½ cup yellow cornmeal
3 teaspoons baking powder
2 teaspoons sugar

¼ teaspoon salt
½ cup cold butter
½ cup shredded Cheddar cheese
1 cup milk

Preheat oven to 450°. In a large bowl, combine flour, cornmeal, baking powder, sugar and salt. Cut in butter until mixture is crumbly. Stir in cheese and milk until moistened. Drop by ¼ cupfuls, 2 inches apart into an ungreased baking sheet. Bake 12 to 15 minutes until light golden brown. Serve warm. Serves 12.

J.M. Davis Arms & Historical Museum

J.M. Davis

J.M. Davis Arms & Historical Museum

330 North J.M. Davis Boulevard • Claremore
918-341-5707 • www.thegunmuseum.com

Located in Claremore, on historic Route 66, the J.M. Davis Arms & Historical Museum is the world's largest privately held arms museum.

Featuring over 50,000 unique items including firearms, swords, military weapons, saddles, spurs, World War I posters and movie and TV western memorabilia, the museum is a one of a kind attraction. Waiting to be discovered are outlaw guns, Native American artifacts, John Rogers statuaries, antique music boxes, musical instruments and over 1,200 steins from all over the world.

John Monroe Davis (1887-1973) was seven years old when his father bought him his first gun. Thus began the most famous gun collection in the world.

Davis displayed the collection in a 120 room hotel in downtown Claremore. In 1965 Davis transferred ownership to the J.M. Davis Foundation, Inc., a non-profit trust. The collection was loaned to the state of Oklahoma for 99 years and the state built the current museum to house the collection in 1969.

It remains a popular tourist attraction on America's Highway, Route 66. The museum is open seven days a week from April to October, and closed on Sunday from October to April. Groups are welcome and there is plenty of parking for buses.

Dutch Oven Biscuits

2 cups flour
½ teaspoon salt
3 teaspoons baking powder
4 tablespoons solid shortening
1 cup milk (diluted canned milk is okay)

Blend flour, salt and baking powder. Mash in shortening with a fork until crumbly. Add milk and stir until dough sags down into trough left by spoon as it moves around the bowl. Turn dough out on a floured surface; knead 30 seconds. Pat out gently until ½-inch thick. Cut with a round cutter or pinch off pieces of dough and form by hand. Put biscuits into a greased Dutch oven, cover, and bury in bright coals for 5 or 10 minutes or until golden brown.

Barbara Reich
Deer Festival & Outdoor Show

Out of this World Rolls

2 packages yeast
1¼ cups warm water, divided
3 eggs, well beaten
4 to 5 cups flour

½ cup shortening
½ cup sugar
2 teaspoons salt
Butter

Dissolve yeast in ¼ cup warm water and let stand 10 minutes. Combine yeast, eggs, 2½ cups flour, 1 cup warm water, shortening, sugar and salt in a large bowl. Beat at medium speed until smooth, scraping sides of bowl. Stir in remaining flour to make soft dough; cover. Let rise until double in size, about 1 hour. Punch down and refrigerate overnight. About 3 hours before baking, roll out as desired. Let rise 3 hours until doubled, bake in 400° oven 12 to 15 minutes. Brush tops with butter.

Susan Scott
Holiday in the Park

Cattlemen's Hot Yeast Rolls

1¾ ounces yeast (wet)
2 ounces (4 tablespoons)
  salad oil
1 egg
2½ ounces (⅓ cup) sugar

13 ounces (1½ cups plus
  2 tablespoons) milk
3¾ cups flour
1 teaspoon salt

Put yeast in mixer with wire whip; beat on low seed to break up yeast. Add oil and blend until smooth. Add egg and sugar. Mix on speed #2 until creamy. Remove whip and attach dough hook. Add milk and mix well on low speed. Add flour, then salt. Mix on low speed until flour is wet and blended. Put on speed #2. Let mix until dough has pulled away from bowl. Remove dough from mixing bowl and place in larger bowl to rise. Place in warm area with light and towel on top. Wait for dough to rise double its volume. Punch air out of dough, until it is flat again. Allow dough to rise a second time. Then roll/cut dough into proper sizes. When dough is placed in cooking vessel, allow to rise a third time. When dough has doubled in size again, place in conventional oven on center oven rack at 350° about 20 minutes, or until golden brown.

Historic Stockyards City
Courtesy of Cattlemen's Steakhouse

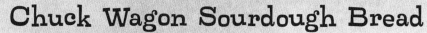

Chuck Wagon Sourdough Bread

This may seem like a lot of trouble, but it sure tastes good!

First, and most important to making sourdough bread, is the Sourdough Starter. The starter can be your best friend or your worst enemy. It's like you treat your kids, if you don't treat them right, they won't behave. Keeping it stirred and fed is important for a good starter.

THE STARTER:

1 package yeast
4 cups water
2 tablespoons sugar
4 cups flour

1 potato, peeled and cut into fourths (you may substitute 1 teaspoon instant potatoes every so often)

Mix all ingredients together, adding the potato last. Stir daily. After 3 to 4 days, you can use it, but the older it gets, the better it is. A brown liquid called hooch comes to the top of the container; just stir it back into the mixture. You can put it into the refrigerator then. Just add 2 tablespoons sugar every 3 days, and 1 tablespoon instant potatoes once a week.

To replenish the starter, add 1 cup flour, 1 cup water, and 3 teaspoons sugar. Add back whatever you take out. For instance, if you use 4 cups starter put back in 2 cups flour, 2 cups water and 6 teaspoons sugar.

THE BREAD:

3 handfuls flour
½ teaspoon salt
1 tablespoon sugar

2 teaspoons baking powder
2 cups Starter

Add first 4 ingredients to a bowl and mix in the Starter; knead. Add more flour as you go to keep dough from sticking. Pour a small amount of oil in a baking pan. Grease your hands and pinch off dough the size of an egg and roll it in the palm of your hands. Arrange the dough balls so that they touch each other in your pan. Make sure balls are rolled in oil as you put them in pan. Bake in a preheated 400° oven about 35 minutes, or until brown.

Julie McKinney
Western Spirit Celebration

Western Spirit Celebration

Third Weekend in September

Chisholm Trail Heritage Center
1000 Chisholm Trail Parkway • Duncan
580-252-6692 • www.onthechisholmtrail.com

Children and adults will be immersed in the western culture, art and heritage of the Chisholm Trail. The Western Spirit Celebration explores the contribution of many multi-ethnic groups and their impact on the economy, culture and nature of the settlement of the West.

Activities include: a longhorn cattle drive, chuck wagon grub, Western artisans, entertainers and vendors, children's games, cowboy poets, stock-dog demonstrations, horse-pulling contest and more.

Come to the event and receive free admission to the Chisholm Trail Heritage Center, named by *True West Magazine* as one of the Top 10 Best Western Museums in the country.

Quick White Bread

2 cups lukewarm water
2 tablespoons yeast (2 packages)
3 tablespoons sugar
1½ teaspoons salt
3 tablespoons oil
1 egg
2 tablespoons water
6 to 8 cups flour

Mix 2 cups water and yeast together. Let set until it starts to foam. Add sugar, salt and oil. Beat egg with 2 tablespoons water and add to yeast mixture. Add flour. Work dough on floured breadboard about 10 minutes until it has an elastic texture. Place in a greased bowl and punch down 2 or 3 times when it rises. Work into 2 loaves and place in greased pan. Bake in a 375° for 45 to 50 minutes. If rolls are preferred, form dough into rolls and place in a greased pan and let rise. Bake in a 425° oven 15 to 20 minutes.

Jane Apple
Hitching Post Bed & Breakfast

Fresh Lavender Bread

(BREAD MACHINE RECIPE)

1¼ cups water
2 tablespoons olive oil
3 teaspoons sugar
1 teaspoon salt
1 tablespoon ground lavender
3 cups bread flour
2 teaspoons yeast

Mix well and prepare according to bread machine instructions, basic cycle. Enjoy with lavender spread!

Tip: Ground lavender can be added to any bread recipe. Create some new favorites for your family!

*Country Cottage Primitives
Lavender Farm*

**Country Cottage Primitives
Lavender Farm
Shawnee Convention &
Visitors Bureau**

Fresh Lavender Spread

1 tablespoon ground lavender
1 stick real butter, softened

Blend well, place in container and refrigerator 24 to 36 hours. Enjoy!

**Country Cottage Primitives Lavender Farm
Shawnee Convention & Visitors Bureau**

Mexican Cornbread

½ cup margarine
¼ to ½ cup sugar
4 eggs
1 can chopped green
   chiles

1 can cream-style corn
2 cups shredded cheese
1 cup flour
1 cup self-rising cornmeal
½ cup chopped onion

Preheat oven to 350°. Mix all ingredients together and bake 1 hour.

Kathy Blakley
Heartland Cruise Car Show

Often referred to as "The Mother Road," Route 66 was born in Oklahoma. Today, this historic highway pays nostalgic homage to a time gone by with a wealth of roadside attractions and iconic symbols of American folklore.

Heartland Cruise Car Show

Father's Day Weekend

Downtown Weatherford
580-772-7744 • toll-free 800-725-7744
www.weatherfordchamber.com

Come Cruise on Historic Route 66!

Every Father's Day kicks off the Heartland Cruise Car Show. Over 250 classic cars cruise down Route 66 on Friday evening and are displayed on Saturday at Weatherford's Rader Park. Everything from early model Mustangs, T-Birds, Corvettes, trucks, street rods and motorcycles will gleam throughout the day.

Do you like riding motorcycles? Do you like playing poker? Well, play poker while riding in the $1000 Poker Run. The Run begins at 8:00 am with the last card being turned at 10:00 am at Rader Park. Come out, see the cars, and enjoy the remembrances of a more innocent time in America's history.

When surfing the web, be sure to "Like" them on Facebook.

Pumpkin Pancakes
at Aaron's Gate Country Getaways

1 egg
1 (30-ounce) can Libby's
   Pumpkin Pie Mix

⅓ cup cooking oil
4 cups Bisquick
Water

Beat egg slightly. Add pumpkin pie mix and oil. Fold in Bisquick. Add water till consistency of pancake batter (pours easily but not runny). Heat griddle to 350°. Lightly oil griddle. Using a ¼ cup measure, pour pancake batter on griddle. Bake approximately 3 minutes on each side. Be careful not to burn as these pancakes are very moist and take longer to cook. Garnish with chopped apple, syrup, chopped pecans and a sprinkle of brown sugar.

Aaron's Gate Country Getaways

Aaron's Gate Country Getaways
Bed & Breakfast

Guthrie

405-282-0613 • 877-540-1300

www.aaronsgate.com

Nestled near the middle of the state is Aaron's Gate Country Getaways Bed & Breakfast. Boasting luxurious honeymoon cottages for two in the country, Aaron's Gate provides both opulence and privacy. There are three unique cottages with the amenities of a five-star resort: Jacuzzis for two, gas fireplaces, European Spa Showers, full-kitchens, screened porches with hot tubs and dry saunas, surround-sound TV/VCR/DVD, robes, bath amenities and refreshments. Aaron's Gate is a sister to the famous Arcadian Inn and serves the same delicious breakfast with "to die for" Vanilla Butter Sauce.

Great packages can be arranged to enhance your getaway including a couple massage in your cottage, dinner basket, flowers, a Babymoon and much more. Visit their website for more information.

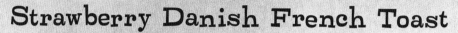

Strawberry Danish French Toast

STRAWBERRY FREEZER JAM:

2 cups crushed strawberries (1 quart fully ripe strawberries)

4 cups sugar

1 box Sure-Jell fruit pectin

¾ cup water

Rinse 5 (1-cup) plastic containers and lids with boiling water. Dry thoroughly. Stem and crush strawberries thoroughly, 1 cup at a time. Measure exactly 2 cups prepared fruit into large bowl. Stir in sugar. Let stand 10 minutes, stirring occasionally. Mix water and pectin in small saucepan. Bring to boil over high heat, stirring constantly. Continue boiling and stirring 1 minute. Add to fruit mixture; stir 3 minutes or until sugar is almost dissolved. (A few sugar crystals may remain.)

Fill containers immediately to within ½ inch of tops. Wipe off top edges of containers; immediately cover with lids. Let stand at room temperature 24 hours. Jam is now ready to use. Store in refrigerator up to 3 weeks or in freezer up to 1 year. Thaw in refrigerator before using.

FRENCH TOAST:

3 eggs

1 cup milk

2 tablespoons sugar

1 teaspoon cinnamon

1 teaspoon vanilla

4 slices Italian bread

1 package cream cheese, softened

Powdered sugar

Strawberry Freezer Jam

Heat griddle to 400°. Beat eggs and milk, sugar, cinnamon and vanilla. Dip each slice of bread into the egg mixture and place on hot greased griddle. Cook 1 to 2 minutes till browned and flip over. Spread about 1 tablespoon cream cheese on 2 slices. Cook another 1 to 2 minutes till brown on other side. Set browned French toast slice on top of creamed cheese slice like a sandwich. Place on plate. Sprinkle with powdered sugar and top with Strawberry Freezer Jam.

Aaron's Gate Country Getaways

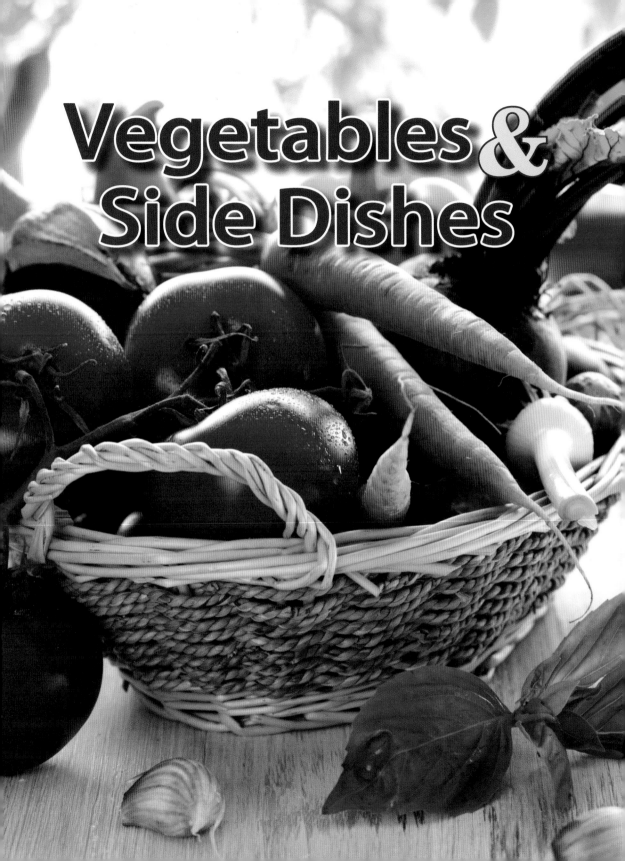

Vegetables & Side Dishes

Baked Beans

1 large onion, chopped
1 cup brown sugar
½ cup white vinegar
½ teaspoon garlic salt
½ teaspoon salt
½ teaspoon dry mustard
1 can Bush's baked beans, NOT drained

1 can ranch-style beans, NOT drained
1 can butter beans, drained
1 can pork and beans, drained
1 can green beans, drained (French style or cut)
4 strips bacon

Preheat oven to 325°. Place onion, brown, sugar, vinegar, garlic salt, salt and dry mustard in a saucepan; cover and cook 20 minutes over medium heat. Place all beans in a large mixing bowl. Stir together. Pour onion and spice mixture over beans and stir. Place bean mixture in a 3-quart casserole dish and place strips of bacon on top. Bake 45 minutes.

Delyn Cronk
The Dehydrator

The Dehydrator

Last Saturday in July

Simmons Center
800 Chisholm Trail Parkway • Duncan
580-439-4827 • www.thedehydrator.org
www.facebook.com/pages/The-Dehydrator/186385604720336

Founded in 1990, The Dehydrator has become one of Oklahoma's premier cycling events. Officially endorsed by the Oklahoma Governor's Council on Physical Fitness and Sports, The Dehydrator offers participants their choice of either a fun ride or a professionally timed citizens race. The fun ride offers distances of 10, 25, 50, and 62 miles typically heading south of Duncan towards scenic Waurika Lake and back. The physically demanding race is held north of Duncan, around area lakes, and is comprised of multiple laps of 14 miles, depending on age and gender brackets. The event is staged at Duncan's wonderful Simmons Center recreation facility where entrants can enjoy 'run of the house', including showers, pool, saunas, and gym equipment. A delish-i-o-so meal is included and served up around noon, along with medals and jerseys for the racers. The event is sponsored by the Duncan Band Boosters, and proceeds go to support the local band programs, as well as supplying new bicycles for the Toy Shop Christmas drive. The Dehydrator is 'Always the Last Saturday in July'. All riders agree: The Dehydrator is a 'must do' event!

Bacon Spice Green Beans

2 slices bacon, chopped
1 small onion, chopped
1 garlic clove, minced

⅛ teaspoon red pepper flakes
1½ cups green beans, drained
¼ cup beef broth

Preheat large skillet. Add bacon and cook until brown; transfer to plate, reserving drippings in skillet. Sauté onions and garlic in bacon drippings until soft. Add red pepper, green beans and broth; cover and continue to cook, stirring occasionally, until beans are wilted and soft. Stir in bacon and serve.

Carolyn Petty
The Dehydrator

"Bundle Up" Green Beans

¼ cup butter
¼ cup brown sugar
½ pound sliced bacon
1 to 2 cans whole green beans
Toothpicks

Melt butter and brown sugar together. Set aside. Cut bacon slices in half across. Drain beans. Gather 5 to 6 beans together and wrap with bacon. Secure with toothpick. Place on rimmed baking sheet. Cook at 375° until bacon is crisp and done, about 30 minutes. Last 5 minutes, pour sugar mixture over beans and return to oven.

Courtesy of Santa's Old Broads
Pelican Festival

Alabaster Caverns State Park

The largest natural gypsum cave in the world open to the public is located in Freedom at Alabaster Caverns State Park. Daily tours offer visitors the opportunity to learn of the caves prize mineral and to see amazing selenite formations. In addition to caves, the park has numerous hiking trails. With varying degrees of difficulty, each trail is home to wildlife and distinctive vegetation.

Chickasaw Frittata

10 eggs
1 cup sour cream
2 tablespoons freshly chopped
  cilantro
Salt and pepper to taste
1 (15.5-ounce) can black beans,
  rinsed and drained

1 (15.5-ounce) can yellow hominy,
  drained
1 (10-ounce) can diced tomatoes
  with green chiles, drained
1 cup shredded Monterey Jack
  cheese
1 cup shredded Cheddar cheese

Preheat oven to 350°. Spray a 9x13-inch baking dish with nonstick cooking spray. In a large bowl, beat eggs and sour cream until smooth. Add cilantro, salt, pepper, beans, hominy, tomatoes with green chiles and Monterey Jack cheese. Stir mixture until thoroughly mixed. Pour into sprayed baking dish. Sprinkle Cheddar cheese on top. Place baking dish in oven and bake approximately 1 hour. Frittata will be evenly firm on top when done.

Montford Inn

Montford Inn

322 West Tonhawa • Norman
405-321-2200 • www.montfordinn.com

In the heart of Norman, Oklahoma, near the University of Oklahoma, Montford Inn Bed and Breakfast is an experience of the comfort of home, while being a part of something special.

Montford Inn Bed and Breakfast is everything the discriminating guest has come to expect: Elegance, comfort, charm, attention to detail, antiquity and location. Guests will find the spirit of the Inn to be delightfully romantic and relaxing.

The Murray family built the inn in 1994, and designed it to create a unique quality and personalized atmosphere, achieving a distinctive ambiance through a combination of elegance and country tradition. With ten guestrooms with bathrooms in the main inn and six cottage suites across the street, the Montford offers many different options for guests.

Crescent Veggie Squares

1 (8-ounce) package refrigerated crescent rolls
1 (8-ounce) package cream cheese, softened
1 (1-ounce) package Ranch-style dressing mix (dry)
2 carrots, finely chopped
½ cup chopped cauliflower
½ cup chopped broccoli
½ cup chopped green onions

Preheat oven to 375°. Roll out crescent rolls onto baking sheet. Stretch and flatten to form a single rectangular shape. Bake until golden brown. Allow to cool. Place cream cheese in a bowl. Mix cream cheese with ranch dressing mix. Spread mixture over cooled crust. Arrange vegetables on top. Chill 1 hour. Cut into bite-size squares.

Jane Apple
Hitching Post Bed & Breakfast

The state flag honors the rich history and contributions of Native Americans in Oklahoma. The blue field signifies devotion, the shield is a symbol of defensive or protective warfare, but always surmounted by the olive branch and peace pipe which betoken the love of peace by a united people. Crosses on the shield are Native American signs for stars, representing high ideals.

Maque Choux Corn

4 cups whole-kernel field corn (MUST be field corn.
   Sweet corn will NOT work.)
¼ cup olive oil
1 small can Rotel tomatoes (original)

Cook all ingredients together over medium heat in a
heavy skillet until sticky. Serve warm.

Buffalo Creek Guest Ranch

Good n' Easy
Corn Casserole

1 (16-ounce) can whole-kernel corn
2 (16-ounce) cans cream-style corn
1 stick butter
1 cup sour cream
1 (8.5-ounce) package cornbread mix

Mix ingredients together and place in
casserole dish. Bake at 350° for 1 hour.

Virginia Scott
Holiday in the Park

*Allan Houser's magnificent bronze
sculpture, "Unconquered," stands
watch, facing the rising sun every
day. The statue was installed at the
Oklahoma History Center in 2005,
the year it opened.*

Grandma's Corn Casserole

3 eggs, lightly beaten
½ cup oil
¾ cup cornmeal
¾ cup milk
2 cans Rotel, drained (mild or hot)
1 pound grated sharp Cheddar cheese

1 can cream corn
1 can whole-kernel corn, drained
¾ teaspoon salt
¾ teaspoon baking soda
2 tablespoons flour
6 green onions, chopped

Preheat oven to 375°. Place all ingredients in a large mixing bowl. Mix. Pour into a buttered casserole dish and bake 35 minutes.

Cathy Clement
Chisholm Trail Historical Preservation Society, Inc.

Chisholm Trail
Crawfish Festival

June

Kirkpatrick Farm
1001 Garth Brooks Boulevard • Yukon
405-350-8937
www.chisholmtrail.org

Yukon's annual Chisholm Trail Festival is a fun filled weekend combining old west living history and a crawfish festival!

Stroll through the historical encampments and visit reenactors, chuck wagon cooks, cowboys, settlers, blacksmiths, gunfighters, military camps and the sutleries. Pull up a hay bale and relax! Have a cold sarsaparilla at the saloon, visit the Saddle Shop, Parker Station, Sheriff Hoppy's Jail, General Store and Nellies, or go to the old school house when you hear the bell ring!

Enjoy the Kreative Korral, train rides, pony rides, clowns, petting zoo, potting shed and more. Leave the old west and venture into the history of this area during the Louisiana Purchase. A taste of Louisiana under Chef Clint Eaves' supervision provides numerous Cajun dishes and pots of boiled crawfish and all the fixins! The sounds of live Cajun and blues music cannot be overlooked. Compete in the crawfish eating contest, chicken scramble, crawfish race, pie eating and cornbread and beans contests. Visit various food booths, craft booths and numerous demonstrations.

Top all this off with a craft show and numerous demonstrations for a perfect weekend in Yukon, hosted by the Chisholm Trail Historical Preservation Society and the City of Yukon.

Cheesy Cauliflower Rice Casserole

1 cup dry rice
1 head cauliflower, chopped and washed
1 egg
¼ stick butter
¼ cup flour
2 cups milk, 2% or whole is best
2 teaspoons dry mustard
1 to 2 teaspoons seasoning salt
3 cups shredded sharp Cheddar cheese, more to taste
½ teaspoon pepper

Cook rice according to package directions and steam cauliflower. While rice and cauliflower are cooking, crack egg into a small bowl and beat lightly. Put butter and flour in the bottom of a large pot and stir constantly over medium-low heat, for 3 to 5 minutes, until fragrant and foamy. Add milk and stir until smooth. Let cook 3 to 5 minutes until thickened. Add mustard and seasoning salt. Take ¼ cup hot milk mixture and slowly add it to egg, stirring constantly. Add egg mixture to big pot and stir until smooth. Add 2 cups cheese to the pot, continuing to stir until smooth. In a casserole dish, add rice and cauliflower. Season with pepper and mix together. Pour cheese mixture over top and toss. Top with cheese and serve.

Christie Greeson
Enid Lights Up the Plains

Corn Casserole

1 can whole-kernel corn
1 can creamed corn
8 ounces cream cheese
¼ cup rice
¼ teaspoon garlic powder

½ teaspoon salt
¼ teaspoon pepper
1 teaspoon onion powder
Bacon bits to taste

Preheat oven to 350°. Prepare rice per directions. In a separate saucepan, cook corn, whole-kernel and creamed, and cream cheese until cheese melts. Add rice and seasoning; mix. Pour into a casserole dish and sprinkle with bacon bits. Bake 30 minutes. Makes 4 servings.

Historic Stockyards City
"Centennial Cookbook" (2010)

Pickled Black-Eyed Peas

2 cans black-eyed peas
1 cup salad oil
¼ cup wine vinegar

1 clove garlic
½ cup thinly sliced onion
½ teaspoon salt

Drain black-eyed peas and place in a bowl. Add remaining ingredients. Store in refrigerator at least 2 days—remove garlic clove after 1 day. Will keep for a week and will continue to improve. Serve warm on New Year's Day for luck or riches for the rest of the year.

from Tom's lovely Mother, June
Redbud Ridge Vineyard & Winery

Squash Medley

2 cups white scallop squash
3 cups yellow squash
3 cups zucchini squash
1 large onion
3 tomatoes
1 sweet green bell pepper

½ pound Velveeta cheese, diced
4 to 5 slices white bread, buttered, toasted, and crumbled for breadcrumbs

Dice squash and onions and cook in salted water a few minutes. Drain and add remaining ingredients. Put in large greased casserole in layers with cheese and breadcrumbs. Bake at 350° until cheese is melted.

Colita Murray's Great Grandmother Hayes
Enid Lights Up the Plains

Enid Lights Up the Plains

The Friday after Thanksgiving

Downtown Square • Enid
580-234-1052
www.mainstreetenid.org

Enid Lights Up The Plains, sponsored by Park Avenue Thrift, is Enid's annual premier special event, drawing thousands of people downtown to see the square outlined in white lights, to visit Santa, take a horse drawn carriage ride around the square, listen to live Christmas music, and watch a fabulous fireworks finale choreographed to Christmas music. The event takes place the Friday after Thanksgiving, and has become Enid's traditional "kick-off to the Christmas season". The event is free to the public. There are food vendors on the Courthouse lawn and children are entertained by elves while waiting in line to talk to Santa. Elementary schools from Enid "adopt" trees on the Courthouse lawn to decorate. These are judged based on originality, creativity and neatness. First, second and third place winners are given cash prizes and are announced from the gazebo during the event. The fireworks have increased in length and quality each year, thanks to our great partnership with Western Enterprises!

The purpose of this event is to provide a hometown Christmas experience for the entire community.

Turnips Au Gratin

3 cups julienne turnip slices (smaller turnips are less likely to be bitter than very large ones)
1 tablespoon sugar
1 (8-ounce) carton sour cream
1 can cream of chicken soup
1 soup can milk
1¼ sticks butter, chunks (divided)

1½ cups grated Cheddar cheese, divided
1 teaspoon salt
1 teaspoon garlic powder
Dried parsley and pepper to taste
1 large onion, thinly sliced
French fried onion rings

Combine turnips with sugar and set aside. Combine sour cream, soup and milk; stir well. Stir in 1 stick butter and 1 cup cheese. Add seasonings. Mix together with turnips and sliced onions. Pour into baking dish. Top with remaining grated cheese and remaining ¼ stick butter. Bake at 350° till bubbly and browned, 45 minutes to 1 hour. Sprinkle with French fried onion rings (can substitute buttered bread or cracker crumbs). Return to oven until topping is browned.

June McGee
Prize-Winning Recipe from the 2011 Turnip Cook-Off
Turnip Festival

Turnip Festival

November

Historic Armory building, 2nd and Kansas
Downtown Cherokee
580-701-4704

Cherokee, the county seat for Alfalfa County, in Northwest Oklahoma is a great place to visit, and an even better place to call home. A traditional farming and ranching community, it is fast becoming known for oil and gas production as well. Cherokee is famous for its family events, with an all day Fourth of July, great community support for its athletic teams and 4H and FFA youth. When Cherokee Main Street decided to add a fall downtown festival to its calendar of events, it wanted something that celebrated their rural heritage and provided fun for all ages. The theme for the festival was found in a poem by an anonymous pioneer who made the land run of 1893. To this day, many farmers in Alfalfa county plant turnips each fall. Even after the record setting drought of 2011 there were still plenty of turnips to decorate, make race cars, shoot from guns, and even eat! A pedal tractor pull and wagon rides further celebrate Cherokee's rural heritage. A free concert and dance is a perfect finish to the evening!

Check out the humorous and festival-inspiring poem on page 254.

Turnips, Celery and Tomatoes

4 turnips, peeled and sliced
2 cups chopped celery
2 tablespoons butter

4 tomatoes, chopped
3 cups water
Seasonings to taste

Simmer turnips and celery in butter over low heat. Add remaining ingredients and simmer, covered, for 15 to 20 minutes.

Carolyn Stands
Turnip Festival

Turnips in Dijon Sauce

2 medium turnips, peeled and
   chopped
1 medium potato, peeled and
   chopped
1 carrot, chopped
1 stalk celery, chopped

1 onion, chopped
½ cup mayonnaise
1 tablespoon Dijon mustard
1 tablespoon lemon juice
Freshly ground pepper

Steam vegetables for 10 minutes. In a separate saucepan, combine mayonnaise, mustard, lemon juice and pepper and heat gently. Add vegetables to sauce and stir to coat. Serve immediately. Serves 4 to 6.

Marcia Brown
Turnip Festival

Smoky Good Onions

3 large sweet onions (Vidalia or Maui)
Oil
4 tablespoons butter, softened
1 teaspoon Worcestershire sauce

Peel onions and slice off the non-root end. With a spoon, hollow out onion. Rub onions with oil. Combine butter and Worcestershire. Place an equal amount into each onion. Wrap tightly in foil and place on smoker or grill for 45 minutes. Serves 6.

Oklahoma Championship Steak Cook-Off

Creamed Cabbage with Caraway

1 head cabbage, washed and chopped

Salt
2 tablespoons butter

CREAM SAUCE:

2 tablespoons flour (more or less flour depending on amount of liquid on cabbage)

½ to ¾ cup cream
1 teaspoon caraway seed

Place cabbage in large saucepan. Add salt to taste, and add enough water to cover. Cook slowly until cabbage is soft. Drain excess water, if necessary, leaving enough for cabbage to barely float. Add butter. Combine cream sauce ingredients; mix well. Stir into cabbage and continue to cook until heated through.

Kolache Festival

Dandelion Greens and Potatoes

4 quarts freshly picked dandelion greens
¼ pound salt pork
8 medium potatoes, peeled and quartered
Salt and pepper
Butter

Wash greens. Drain. Tear into pieces. Chop salt pork into ½-inch chunks. Boil water in large saucepan. Add greens and salt pork. Cover and simmer 1½ hours. Drop in potatoes the last ½ hour. When potatoes are done, drain. Pour into serving dish. Salt and pepper and top with butter slices.

Harn Homestead & 1889ers Museum

Harn Homestead & 1889ers Museum

1721 North Lincoln Boulevard
Oklahoma City
405-235-4058
www.harnhomestead.com

Step back in time at the Historic Harn Homestead Museum. An Oklahoma treasure, the Harn Homestead & 1889ers Museum celebrates the territorial history of Oklahoma, offering a "hands-on" and "minds-on" experience.

Visitors share in the abundance of a territorial farm, the brilliance of a one-room school house, the grace of a Victorian home, and the waste-not want-not ethic of a territorial farm family. There is no place else in Oklahoma that can offer this experience which captures the spirit of the brave men, women, and children who settled this state.

Learn about the territorial life of Oklahoma. This beautiful outdoor museum is original Land Run property and home to some of the most unique treasures of Oklahoma's past. Schedule your visit today and reminisce about days gone by and the traditions of Oklahoma's early settlers.

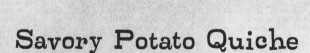

Savory Potato Quiche

3 cups frozen hash-brown potatoes
⅓ cup butter, melted
1 cup chopped cooked ham
1 cup shredded Cheddar cheese
¼ cup chopped bell pepper

¼ cup finely chopped onion
1 jalapeño, finely chopped (optional)
2 eggs
½ cup milk
Salt and pepper to taste

Preheat oven to 425°. Pat potatoes over bottom and up sides of an ungreased 9-inch pie plate. Pour butter over potatoes. Bake 25 minutes. Remove potatoes and reduce oven temperature to 350°. Layer ham, cheese, bell pepper, onion and jalapeño on crust. In a separate bowl, mix eggs, milk, salt and pepper until well blended and pour over layers. Bake 25 minutes.

Oklahoma History Center

Aerial view of Oklahoma History Center

Oklahoma History Center

800 Nazih Zuhdi Drive • Oklahoma City
405-522-0765 • www.okhistorycenter.org

Mon – Sat 10 am to 5 pm

The Oklahoma History Center explores the unique people and stories of Oklahoma's past, present and future. Five galleries and three outdoor exhibits tell Oklahoma's story; oil and gas to aviation; Dust Bowl to space exploration; tornadoes to the Land Run; Native American Indians to Route 66, stories of triumph and tragedy, hope and heartache, famous and infamous.

The Oklahoma History Center is a testament to the indomitable spirit that built Oklahoma. Four permanent galleries and a special exhibits hall showcase the more than 200 hands-on interactives and 50 subjects that tell the stories of Oklahoma and its people.

Conveniently located in the Capital Complex, the Oklahoma History Center is adjacent to the State Capital and the Governor's Mansion, both within easy driving or walking distance. The History Center is conveniently located off of I-35 and I-40. Easy passenger pick-up, drop-off and free motorcoach parking.

The Winnie Mae Café located inside the Oklahoma History Center, offers fresh, made-to-order gourmet soups, salads, sandwiches and entrées.

Bacon and Tomato Quiche

4 ounces Swiss cheese, grated
4 ounces Provolone, grated
8 ounces Cheddar, grated
¾ cup chopped fresh tomato
6 strips bacon, cooked crisp and
    crumbled

¼ cup thin sliced green onion
5 large eggs
½ cup milk
½ cup Bisquick
Salt and pepper to taste
Tabasco sauce to taste

Preheat oven to 350°. In a 9-inch quiche pan or pie plate, layer cheeses over bottom. Sprinkle tomatoes, bacon and onion on top of cheese. In a mixing bowl, beat eggs; add in milk, Bisquick, salt, pepper and Tabasco sauce. Pour over vegetables and cheeses. Bake 45 minutes. Remove and let stand 10 minutes. Serves 8.

Aaron's Gate Country Getaways

10-Gallon Hash Brown Casserole

1 (30-ounce) package frozen
   shredded hash browns,
   partially thawed
1 cup sour cream
1 cup butter, melted (divided)

2 cans cream of chicken soup
1 onion, diced
50 to 60 round buttery
   crackers, crushed

Preheat oven to 350°. Combine hash browns, sour cream, ½ cup butter, soup and onion in a large bowl and mix thoroughly. Spread in a greased 9x13-inch baking dish. In a separate bowl, pour remaining butter over crushed crackers and toss gently. Sprinkle over potato mixture. Bake 1 hour.

Nutty Sweet Potatoes

4½ cups sweet potatoes,
   cooked and mashed
1½ cups sugar

3 eggs, beaten
¾ teaspoon vanilla
¾ cup margarine

Mix together and pour into a 9x13-inch pan.

TOPPING:

1½ cups brown sugar
½ cup margarine, melted

¾ cup flour
1½ cups chopped nuts

Mix and sprinkle over mashed potatoes. Bake at 350° for 30 minutes.

Karolyn Anders
Holiday in the Park

Cowboy Potatoes

6 slices bacon
8 baked potatoes, chopped
1 onion, chopped

½ green pepper, diced
Salt and pepper to taste

Fry bacon and remove from pan. In bacon grease, fry potatoes, onion and green pepper until tender. Cut bacon in pieces and add to mixture. Add salt and pepper.

Pawnee Bill Museum and Original Wild West Show

Pawnee Bill Museum and Original Wild West Show

Come see the show on Saturdays in June!

Pawnee Bill Ranch & Museum
1141 Pawnee Bill Road • Pawnee
918-762-2513 • www.pawneebillranch.com

History comes alive at the Pawnee Bill Ranch, a 500-acre working ranch and historic site located in the beautiful rolling hills of north-central Oklahoma. The ranch was once the home of world-renowned wild west showman, Gordon W. "Pawnee Bill" Lillie and his family. Visitors to the ranch can tour his fully-furnished historic home, blacksmith shop, log cabin, and museum. The Pawnee Bill Ranch is also home to a herd of bison, longhorn, and 4 draft horses. The ranch produces a reenactment of Pawnee Bill's Original Wild West Show every June on the site. Stagecoaches roll amid the thunder of horse hooves as cast members stage an elaborate tribute to the roots of Western entertainment – the Wild West Show. The ranch accommodates tour groups and can provide educational programs to reserved guests. Program options include a bison tour, cowboy whip act, blacksmithing demonstrations, and frontier games. A visit to Oklahoma wouldn't be complete without a trip to the Pawnee Bill Ranch – where the Wild West remains!

Mashed Potatoes with a Twist

3½ cups chicken broth
5 potatoes, peeled and cut into
  1-inch pieces

½ cup light cream
2 tablespoons butter
Black pepper to taste

Add potatoes to chicken broth in a large saucepan; bring to a boil. Reduce heat to medium, cover, and cook until potatoes are tender. Drain, reserving broth. Mash the potatoes with ¼ cup reserved broth, cream, butter and black pepper. Add additional broth for desired consistency. Serve with your favorite gravy.

Durant Main Street

*Magnolia Festival
Durant Main Street*

Durant Main Street

Downtown Durant
580-924-1550 • www.durantmainstreet.org

Right off of I-75 in the southern part of the state is Durant, and it is worth your while to take a stop. There are several things happening in this quaint town throughout the year. Take a look…

Durant is the City of Magnolias, and the town celebrates life at the Magnolia Festival. During the first week in June, stop by and join in on games and festivities for a great family weekend. Ride the ferris wheel and other rides at the carnival, visit all types of crafts and exhibitors, enjoy the live entertainment, and the free children's events!

If you're a runner and are ready for a race, then Colton's Main Street Run should be on your calendar. The race honors the memory of Colton Sherrill, a boy who dearly loved his family, community and playing sports. He began volunteering before he was 5 with Durant Main Street. Colton's Main Street Run benefits the Colton Sherrill Memorial Fund and Durant Main Street. Funds are ear-marked for community projects, scholarships to local students for post high school education, the purchase of Automatic External Defibrillators for sporting venues and local schools, and bleachers for "Colton's Field" at the Durant Sports Complex.

Not a runner? How about a dancer? Taking its cue from the hit reality/dancing television show, Durant Main Street hosts a Dancing with the Stars of Durant fundraiser at the Choctaw Casino Resort's Center Stage. Community leaders and news anchors are paired with area dancers to provide an evening of entertainment that includes fine dining, a silent auction, and an open dance floor.

Contact Durant Main Street for more information on the town, its events, and exciting developments happening throughout each year.

Foil Wrapped Potatoes

10 to 12 potatoes, scrubbed
  and sliced
2 bell peppers (red, green or
  both), chopped

2 onions, chopped
Garlic powder to taste
Salt and pepper to taste
Butter or margarine

Layer potatoes, bell peppers, onions and spices on a large sheet of aluminum foil and dot with butter. (Double foil for extra strength.) Repeat 2 to 3 times until all potatoes have been used. Top with more foil and crimp edges to seal. Cook on a grill or in coals of a fire ring, turning frequently to prevent burning, usually 60 to 90 minutes. This recipe is also excellent cooked in a frying pan for breakfast. Just cut down the quantity and stir all together.

Linda Osburn
Sequoyah Fest & Made in Oklahoma Festival

An aerial photo of
Sequoyah State Park
and Fort Gibson Lake

Sequoyah Fest & Made in Oklahoma Festival

Third Saturday in April

Sequoyah State Park
Hulbert
800-368-1486
www.oklahomaparks.com

Kick off spring at the Sequoyah State Park with Sequoyah Fest. Held on the shores of Fort Gibson Lake, there are paddle boat rides, pony rides, inflatable jumps, nature programs, an archery contest, and basketball shoot-out. Delicious food from a variety of vendors and a concert in the park top off the day.

Within the park is Western Hills Guest Ranch, and on display inside are the goods and wares available for Made In Oklahoma. Quality is the earmark of all Made In Oklahoma products, and the Sequoyah Fest is a great opportunity to support these local artisans.

Delicious Pasta Bake with Veggies

8 ounces angel hair pasta
4 egg whites
1 cup shredded Parmesan
    cheese
½ cup ricotta cheese
1 tablespoon dried basil

1 tablespoon olive oil
2 cups sliced zucchini
1 cup chopped onion
2 cups chopped tomatoes
1½ tablespoons Italian seasoning
4 slices mozzarella cheese

Cook pasta according to directions. In a large bowl, mix together egg whites, Parmesan cheese, ricotta cheese and basil. Toss with cooked pasta and set aside. Heat olive oil in skillet. Sauté zucchini and onion for 6 minutes; add tomatoes and Italian seasoning. Sauté about 2 more minutes. Grease a casserole dish and pour in half of the pasta, then layer veggie mixture and top with 2 slices of mozzarella. Repeat. Bake at 350° for 30 to 35 minutes. Serve warm.

Cross Bar Ranch

Cross Bar Ranch

Located near Turner Falls Park • Davis
In the heart of the Arbuckle Mountains
Exit 55 off I-35, then 1 mile west to Dolese Road and 3 miles south.
580-369-2444 • www.crossbarranch.com

Cross Bar Ranch is a 6500-acre Extreme Ranch. What exactly is an Extreme Ranch? Trail rides with ATVs and Motorcycles instead of horses, that's what! Set in a true wilderness setting, the trails begin fairly easy, giving guests the opportunity to take in the abundant flora and fauna. As the trails progress, so does the degree of difficulty, making headgear and boots a must. The terrain is beautiful and peaceful, a true example of Oklahoma natural beauty.

Primitive camping and RV hookups are available. Call or visit the website for hours and rates.

Mama's Ravioli

12 extra-large eggs, divided
1 tablespoon oil
5 cups all-purpose flour
2 pounds ricotta cheese

Parsley, salt and pepper to taste
¾ cup grated Parmesan
¾ pound mozzarella, shredded

To make dough, beat 9 eggs; add oil. Add flour, a little at a time, mixing well. Knead dough on floured surface. When well-kneaded, place in plastic bag or wrap in plastic and rest 30 minutes or longer. This will allow dough to be more pliable. During this time prepare filling.

Beat 3 eggs until smooth; add ricotta cheese and mix well. Add parsley, salt and pepper; stir in grated Parmesan cheese. Add mozzarella a little a time, mixing well after each addition. This makes a smooth mixture with fewer lumps to tear pasta dough. Cover filling and set aside.

Cut dough into 6 to 8 ribbons and roll out each section in a pasta machine roller set on the thickest setting. Lay rolled strips on a floured surface, or stack with floured waxed paper between each layer. Roll out each dough strip a second time on the next thickest setting. Lay 1 dough strip on a flat floured surface and cut off any rounded or uneven edges. On the top half of the strip, make teaspoon-sized piles of filling set about an inch apart. Dampen dough around each little stack of filling to aid the pressing and cutting process. Fold bottom half dough strip over top, folding very carefully and lightly pressing the edges together around each pile of filling. Press edges together, being careful not to tear dough. Trim off any excess along edge and at ends of strip, but leave enough dough to seal edges with a ravioli cutter. Cut and separate each ravioli, press to seal edges with ravioli tool or fork (seal open edges only; do not seal fold-over edge). Place ravioli on a lightly floured cookie sheet and flash freeze. Freeze each tray in freezer bag until ready to cook. Add frozen ravioli to boiling water, let boil about ten minutes or until ravioli floats to top. Drain and serve with your favorite sauce.

Mark and Bev Nuessle
Rocklahoma

Rocklahoma
Last Weekend in May

Catch the Fever
Festival Grounds
Pryor
866-310-2288
www.rocklahoma.com

Rocklahoma, one of the largest rock festivals in America, returns each year to kick off summer with the nation's largest Memorial Day Weekend party at "Catch the Fever" Music and Festival Grounds located in Pryor, Oklahoma, only 40 minutes northeast of Tulsa!

The "Catch the Fever" festival site is a premier destination for this multi-day festival. On-site facilities include: 4,000 campsites, parking, restrooms, shower houses, a general store for campers, VIP reserved seating area, hospitality areas and much more.

Each year concertgoers from over 30 different countries and all 50 states converge upon the festival grounds for this event.

ROCKLAHOMA was established in 2007 as a classic rock destination festival promoting the motto "life, liberty and the pursuit of rock." ROCKLAHOMA was revamped in 2010 as organizers teamed with AEG Live to create an event encompassing a much broader mix of classic, current and up-and-coming rock artists.

Today, the three-day camp and rock festival features a mix of the best classic bands and today's top active rock artists. Both Playboy and Rolling Stone have cited ROCKLAHOMA as a festival that should not be missed.

Fabulous Macaroni and Cheese

½ pound elbow macaroni
1 teaspoon salt
1 teaspoon pepper
6 tablespoons butter, chunks

1 (16-ounce) package grated
  cheese
1 cup breadcrumbs
1 cup milk

Preheat oven to 350°. In a large pot of boiling water, cook macaroni to al dente; drain and rinse with hot water. Sprinkle with salt and pepper and mix in a 2-quart casserole dish. Layer pasta, butter and cheese. Top final layer of cheese with breadcrumbs. Pour milk over top of breadcrumbs. Bake uncovered 30 minutes. Remove from oven and serve.

Rocklahoma

Green Chile Pepper Casserole

5 eggs
1 cup flour
1½ teaspoon salt
4 cups milk

3 cans green chile peppers
1 pound sharp Cheddar
  cheese

Preheat oven to 350°. Beat eggs and then add flour and salt. Slowly add milk. In a buttered 9x13-inch casserole dish, spread chile peppers and cheese evenly over bottom. Pour in milk and egg mixture. Bake 1 hour. Let casserole rest 5 minutes before serving.

from Tom's lovely Mother, June
Redbud Ridge Vineyard & Winery

Sicilian Sweet Spaghetti Sauce

This sweet spaghetti sauce recipe came to me from a Sicilian woman who used to cook in an Italian restaurant in Manhattan. She says that a young Frank Sinatra regularly requested this sauce upon his frequent visits. It is very simple and, I think, very good.

1 large Spanish or sweet onion, diced
2 cloves garlic, minced
2 tablespoons olive oil
1 large can whole tomatoes, slightly crushed (no seasonings
  added)
3 (12-ounce) cans tomato paste (no seasonings added)
8 to 12 cups water
Sweet basil
1 cup sugar

In a large Dutch oven, over medium heat, mix onion, garlic and oil. Cook until onion is just tender. Add tomatoes, tomato paste and water. Stir until thoroughly mixed. Sprinkle enough sweet basil to make a layer over the top of entire Dutch oven and mix. Add sugar; don't be afraid, the sauce is supposed to taste sweet! (I usually use more than a cup depending on how sour the tomato paste is.) Serve over angel hair or spaghetti.

Johnny Baier
American Banjo Museum

Cumin Rice

⅓ cup chopped onion
¼ cup diced green bell
  pepper
1 cup uncooked rice
2 tablespoons bacon
  drippings (may use oil)

2 (10.5-ounce) cans beef
  consommé
1 tablespoon Worcestershire
  sauce
¾ teaspoon salt
¾ teaspoon cumin powder

Sauté onions, bell pepper and rice in bacon drippings until golden brown. Add consommé, Worcestershire, salt and cumin. Bring to a boil, cover and simmer 20 to 25 minutes.

Arrowhead Resort

Tahlequah

Located in Northeastern Oklahoma in Cherokee County, is the city of Tahlequah. It is the capital of the Cherokee Nation and the United Keetoowah Band of Cherokee Indians.

Unlimited opportunities for outdoor recreation are provided by Lake Tenkiller and Lake Fort Gibson. The beautiful scenery of this part of the state is one-of-a-kind.

Arrowhead Resort

7704 Hwy 10 • Tahlequah
800-749-1140 • 918-456-1140
www.arrowheadresortok.com

October – March: 8 am to noon
April – September: 8 am to 8 pm

Arrowhead Resort possesses a committed, well-trained, helpful, and friendly staff that wants to make each guest's stay as good as possible. Jack Spears and his son David have been deeply involved in this business for years. Jack notes, "We have been servicing people here on the Illinois River for many years now. We know customer service is #1 and that is what we instill in our staff to guarantee your enjoyment with us."

With so many aspects to the resort it is a challenge to mention and show them all! The year-round resort has a General Store with picnic supplies, groceries, dry goods, pop, water, and souvenirs. Arrowhead Resorts has the only Ice Cream Fountain on the river to cool guests off after floating the beautiful Illinois. Professional catering is available upon request and can be set up "on site" before or after a river trip.

Arrowhead Resort is a family oriented business and works hard to go the extra mile on a great many fronts. An extra added bonus is the newly asphalted roads within the camp to eliminate annoying dust! Arrowhead Resort the only operation on or near the river with asphalt roads.

Call or visit the website for reservations or additional information.

Best Ever Baked Rice

1½ cups water
½ cup butter
2 chicken bouillon cubes
2 tablespoons dried minced onion
1 teaspoon dried parsley
1 teaspoon celery seed
¼ teaspoon salt
¾ cup rice, uncooked

Preheat oven to 350°. In a saucepan, bring water to a boil. Add butter, bouillon, onion, parsley, celery seed and salt. Stir until butter is melted; add rice. Pour into a greased casserole dish and cover tightly. Bake 30 minutes. Break up rice with a fork before serving.

Meat & Seafood

Norman's Own Chicken Tenders

A favorite of Jazz in the Park (Jazz in June's Saturday evening concert) for more than a decade. Nothing says picnic in the South like fried chicken. In the interest of a healthier fare, this recipe is for grilled white meat chicken tenders, but can be made with drumsticks, wings, thighs or even prawns.

Basil	Jalapeño pepper sauce
Oregano	Soy sauce
Ground garlic	Lemon juice
Olive oil	3 pounds white meat chicken tenders

Fill a stainless steel bowl about ½ full with a combination of basil, oregano and ground garlic, per your preference. Add olive oil to saturate and bind dry mixture but not drown it. Smash all ingredients together and then mix with a whisk until thoroughly mixed and saturated. Add a few dashes each of jalapeño pepper sauce and soy sauce, and a splash of lemon juice. Mix all ingredients until mixture is spreadable rather than clumpy, but not too wet (consistency of runny pesto).

Spread chicken tenders on baking sheet. Brush thoroughly with mixture, turn and repeat. Reserve remaining mixture.

Apply nonstick spray to grill and bring to high heat. Place chicken tenders on grill. As each side browns to a golden crisp, turn and grill other side. Reapply remaining mixture throughout grilling. Grill until the bits of basil and oregano turn deep brown.

Remove from heat and set aside to cool. Refrigerate overnight or at least a few hours before Jazz in June. Place on a bed of lettuce in a sealable container that can travel safely in a cooler.

Open after everyone has put out side dishes at the picnic, let everyone have a whiff of the spicy aroma and serve from the container. Sit back and enjoy the best jazz in the Southwest as the summer lights fades and the cool breeze sets in for the night!

Norman Hammon
Jazz In June

Jazz in June

June

Thursday and Friday
Brookhaven Village • 3700 West Robinson Street • Norman

Saturday
Andrews Park • 201 West Daws Street • Norman
405-325-3388 • www.jazzinjune.org

For three decades, Jazz in June has been an Oklahoma tradition. Each summer, for three consecutive evenings, world-class musicians take the stage in Norman, filling the air with jazz and blues, plus swing, bebop, salsa, alternative country, contemporary American music and more.

Since its founding in 1984 by the Norman Arts and Humanities Council and the Cimarron Circuit Opera Company, the festival has developed into a much-anticipated annual event attended by some 50,000 people.

In addition to the concerts, Jazz in June includes post-concert blues and jam sessions and a daylong jazz and blues clinic. All events are free and open to the public.

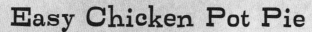

Easy Chicken Pot Pie

1 onion, diced

2 cloves garlic, diced

2 medium potatoes, peeled and
  diced

¼ cup extra virgin olive oil

2 cans chicken stock

2 cups pre-cooked boned and diced
  chicken

1 bag frozen mixed vegetables

1 tablespoon flour

In large soup pan, sauté onion, garlic and potatoes in oil until onion is clear. Add chicken stock and chicken. Cook on high until boiling then add frozen vegetables. Cover and cook on medium ½ hour or until potatoes are soft. Add flour to thicken; stirring occasionally.

I use an extra large version of Favorite Pie Crust (below) putting ½ in deep casserole dish bringing it up and over the sides and baking in 350° oven for 10 minutes. Then pour "stew" into casserole dish until it is about ¾ full and cover with top large layer of pie crust. Pinch together the edges and press fork tines for steam release and pretty presentation. Cook at 350° about 45 minutes or until top crust is nicely browned and you can hear the "stew" sizzling.

Susen Foster, Planet Earth Jewelry

Favorite Pie Crust

Good for sweet or savory dishes.

2 cups unbleached white flour

⅓ cup water

⅔ cup extra virgin olive oil

Mix together until ball forms. Chill for 20 minutes. Cut in half for 2 layers. Roll out ½ between sheets of waxed paper. Put in pan. If you plan to use a filling with short heat time; put pie pan with bottom layer of crust into a 350° oven for 10 minutes. Add filling of choice and continue to heat as needed or roll out top and place over filling. Score as you like and continue to cook.

Susen Foster, Planet Earth Jewelry

Planet Earth Jewelry
by Susen Foster

530 North Pecan Street • Pauls Valley
580-369-8999
www.facebook.com/PlanetEarthJewelrybySusenFoster

Susen Foster says, "I have been blessed with the opportunity to create the kind of jewelry that will get passed on to family members for generations. My necklaces, earrings, bracelets, ankle bracelets, and even horse brow bands and dog collars, are made from God's creations from the sea and shore." Each piece you order from Planet Earth Jewelry is one-of-a-kind. Whether you are buying for yourself or as a gift, this unique jewelry is sure to make the receiver happy.

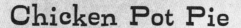

Chicken Pot Pie

1 cup chicken broth
1 package frozen vegetables
1 can cream of chicken soup
Meat from 1 chicken (a
   precooked one is a great
   time saver)

1 stick butter, melted
1 cup milk
1 teaspoon baking powder
1 teaspoon salt
1 cup flour

Preheat oven to 400°. Combine chicken broth, vegetables, soup and meat in a casserole dish and set aside. In a separate bowl, mix together butter, milk, baking powder, salt and flour to make a thick batter. Pour on top of meat mixture. Bake 45 minutes.

Kim Burge
The Dehydrator

Chicken Poppers

3 boneless skinless chicken breasts
1 cup ground fully-cooked ham
25 to 30 pieces cubed Cheddar
   cheese
1 pound sliced bacon

2 to 3 tablespoons olive oil
1 cup chicken broth
½ teaspoon salt
½ teaspoon pepper
Toothpicks

Flatten chicken to ¼-inch thickness, cut into 1½-inch strips. Spread each strip with 1 teaspoon ham. Place cheese cube on end of each strip; roll up. Cut bacon in half, wrap bacon around chicken roll up and secure with toothpick. In large skillet, cook roll-ups in oil until bacon is crispy, about 10 minutes. Add chicken broth, salt and pepper, bring to a boil, reduce heat and simmer 10 to 15 minutes or until chicken is no longer pink. Serve warm. Refrigerate leftovers.

Karen Hill Berkenbile
Enid Lights Up the Plains

Cajun Jambalaya

2 cups diced chicken
8 ounces smoked sausage, sliced thin
1½ cups diced smoked ham
2 cups diced bell pepper and onions
2 cups diced tomatoes, undrained

2 cups chicken broth
1 tablespoon thyme leaves
½ teaspoon salt
2 teaspoons Tony's Creole seasoning
8 ounces medium cooked shrimp
12 ounces rice, parboiled

Spray a 4-quart Dutch oven with cooking spray. Over medium-high heat cook diced chicken, 6 minutes. Add sausage and diced ham. Cook, stirring 2 minutes. Add remaining ingredients; heat to boiling. Reduce heat, cover and simmer 25 minutes.

Clint Eaves
Chisholm Trail Historical Preservation Society, Inc.

Chisholm Trail Park

Boasting a boot walking trail, gazebos, pavilions and a look-out peak, Chisholm Trail Park is a great resting stop. Interconnected with City Park and Freedom Trail Playground, the entire three park area covers 100 acres. The wooded trails are perfect for nature hikes, and there is a playground for the little ones. The Chisholm Trail Park is located at 500 West Vandament Avenue in Yukon.

Chicken Cordon Bleu Casserole

1 cup sour cream
1½ cups chicken broth
1 tablespoon Dijon mustard
¼ teaspoon ground black pepper
1½ cups instant rice, uncooked
4 chicken breasts, cooked and
  chopped

6 slices deli ham, chopped
6 ounces Swiss cheese, chopped
1 cup frozen peas
1 cup corn flakes
½ cup grated Parmesan cheese
2 tablespoons butter, melted

Preheat oven to 400°. Mix together sour cream, chicken broth, mustard and black pepper until smooth. Add rice, chicken, ham, Swiss cheese and peas; mix well. Pour mixture into a greased 9x13-inch baking dish. Combine corn flakes, Parmesan cheese and melted butter in a small bowl and sprinkle over chicken mixture. Bake 25 minutes.

Wright City Lumberjax Festival

Wright City Lumberjax Festival

Second Weekend in October

Wright City Park
Wright City
580-981-2260
www.facebook.com/
WrightCityLumberjaxFestival

The Wright City Lumberjax Festival is an annual, family-oriented event focusing on fun and the proud timber industry of Wright City. Held the second weekend in October, the festival features games, food, live entertainment and vendors of all types of crafts. In addition, forestry events held throughout the day on Saturday provide the opportunity to show off "Lumberjax" credentials. Take a hay ride with one of the town historians and see the sites of this century-old former company town. Grab an Indian taco and peruse the many informational and sales booths or just enjoy listening to the live music.

King Ranch Chicken

Small corn tortillas
5 to 7 bone-in chicken breasts, cooked
1 onion, chopped
½ bell pepper, chopped
1 teaspoon chili powder
1 cup milk

1 can cream of mushroom soup
1 can cream of chicken soup
  (or 2 cans cream of chicken)
1 can Rotel tomatoes
½ pound sharp Cheddar cheese, grated

Conventional oven: Line 9x13-inch pan with broken tortillas and spread chopped chicken over chips. Mix and heat remaining ingredients, except cheese, then pour over chicken. Top with cheese. Cover with foil and bake about 15 minutes; remove foil and bake till cheese bubbles.

12-inch Dutch oven: Layer broken tortillas, chicken and sauce till all is used, top with cheese. Bake with low heat about 15 minutes, then add heat to top till cheese bubbles.

Leigh Ann Matthews
4M Chuck Wagon, Muskogee, OK
Heritage Days: A Living History Festival

Oklahoma Music Hall of Fame and Museum

The Oklahoma Music Hall of Fame and Museum is housed in the Frisco Freight Depot in downtown Muskogee. On an annual basis since 1997, the Oklahoma Music Hall of Fame has been honoring the world's most notable talents whose gifts and musical styles are as breathtaking and diverse as the Oklahoma landscape. In 2003, the Hall of Fame moved into the renovated Frisco Freight Depot to develop a facility honoring the history and legacy of Oklahoma's music, which has contributed so much to the scope of American music.

Heritage Days:
A Living History Festival

September

The Depot District • Muskogee
918-683-2400 • www.downtownmuskogee.com

Downtown Muskogee, Inc. hosts the annual Muskogee Heritage Days: A Living History Festival in the Historic Depot District at Third and Elgin Streets. Join Downtown Muskogee to celebrate the community's rich history. Follow in the footsteps of a legend on the Bass Reeves Legacy Tour. The Tour starts at Three Rivers Museum at 5:30 pm Friday. Costumed interpreters tell the story of one of the most significant lawmen in Indian Territory history.

The Three Rivers Museum and Oklahoma Music Hall of Fame offer Native American dance and song, cowboy and Indian storytellers, an Old West Medicine Show, live music and western crafts and food vendors including Indian tacos, barbecue, hot dogs, popcorn and more. Watch out, 'cause there just might be an attempted train robbery and a shootout at the depot. Antique cars and collectibles, a magic show and vintage games for the kids are all part of the fun.

The afternoon brings fun competitions for visitors to the Depot District including an outrageously fun (and family-friendly) Outhouse Race. An evening concert at the Hall of Fame rounds out Saturday's events.

Peachy Chicken Lettuce Cups

3 ripe (but firm) medium Stratford peaches, peeled, and cut into chunks
1 tablespoon vegetable oil
1 to 2 tablespoons fresh lime juice
2 tablespoons honey
¼ cup finely chopped onion
¼ cup diced green bell pepper
1¼ cups fresh or frozen blueberries
1 teaspoon minced jalapeño pepper
1 tablespoon chopped cilantro
½ teaspoon salt
2 cups cooked and chopped chicken breasts
4 large butter lettuce leaves for garnish
2 to 3 fresh Stratford peaches cut into slices (sprinkle with lime juice to prevent peaches from turning dark)

Combine peaches, vegetable oil, lime juice, honey, onion, bell pepper, blueberries, jalapeño, cilantro, salt and chicken in medium-size bowl. Toss well and let set for an hour to let the flavors meld. Wash lettuce leaves; let dry in refrigerator. On the serving plate, make cups with lettuce leaves and spoon in peach and chicken mixture. Garnish plate with slices of fresh Stratford peaches. Serves 4.

Rosalie Seebeck
Peach Festival

Peach Festival Car Show

Peach Festival

Mid-July

City Park • Stratford
580-759-3700 • www.stratfordok.org

Stratford is known as the Peach Capital of Oklahoma. Since 1906 the Stratford peach has gained a remarkable reputation statewide. In celebration of the many peach growers and orchards, the Stratford Chamber of Commerce hosts an annual festival that has been a growing attraction for over three decades. The morning is kicked off with a free pancake breakfast starting at 6:30 a.m., provided by the Stratford Ministerial Alliance. Also kicking off the festivities is the 5K Bulldog Run, sponsored by the Stratford PTO. There is live entertainment throughout the day from local bands as well as local talent performing in the finals of the Peach Idol. A few other annual events sure to spark interest are the car show, the Peach Royalty contest and the Peach Cook-off. Not only is there fun and games throughout the day for the kids to enjoy, there is also a variety of food, clothing, and arts and crafts vendors from across the state, providing a fun shopping experience for any age. Make room on your calendar to share this fun filled day with family and friends.

Slow Cooker Cranberry Chicken

2½ to 3 pounds skinless chicken thighs

1 (16-ounce) can whole cranberry sauce

2 tablespoons dry onion soup mix

2 tablespoons quick-cooking tapioca

3 cups hot cooked rice

Place chicken in a 3 or 4 quart slow cooker. In a small bowl, stir together cranberry sauce, dry soup mix and tapioca. Pour over chicken. Cover, cook on low setting for 5 or 6 hours. Serve chicken and sauce over hot cooked rice. Yields 6 servings.

Janet Raines
American Banjo Museum

American Banjo Museum

9 East Sheridan Avenue • Oklahoma City
405-604-2793 • www.americanbanjomuseum.com

Tues – Sat 11 am to 6 pm • Sun Noon to 5 pm

*Admission: Adults: $6; Seniors (55+),
Military & Students: $5; Children (6-17):
$4; Children 5 & under: Free*

The American Banjo Museum, located in Oklahoma City's Bricktown Entertainment District, is the only museum in the world dedicated to the preservation and promotion of America's only native musical instrument—the banjo. Come and marvel at the museum's $3.5 million collection of over 300 beautiful and ornately decorated banjos, each one a work of art.

Witness the history of the banjo through interpretive exhibits as well as video and performance—from its humble African roots through its heyday during the Roaring 20s to its present voice in Bluegrass, folk and world music. The elegant galleries on two floors present the sights and sounds of the largest collection of banjos on public display anywhere in the world.

Each year the American Banjo Museum honors the historically significant pioneers of four-string banjo performance, manufacturing and education as well as contemporary artists who carry on the music traditions of their predecessors with an induction ceremony into the National Four String Banjo Hall of Fame. Throughout the year, the museum offers live performances and special concerts, culminating with the Bricktown Banjo Bash held each year throughout the Bricktown Entertainment District.

Cornish Game Hens

1 box chicken flavored Rice-A-Roni
½ stick butter
1 package sliced mushrooms
½ cup slivered almonds

2 cups water
½ cup white wine
4 Cornish hens, whole and cleaned

Sauté rice from Rice-A-Roni box in butter 5 minutes. Add mushrooms and almonds and sauté another 5 minutes. Add water, wine and seasoning packet from box. Place Cornish hens in a baking dish. Stuff each bird with a little rice then pour entire mixture into dish. Cover and bake at 350° till hens are done and juices run clear, about 1½ hours. Remove foil and brown hens.

Donna Rohloff
Premier Lake Property

Premier Lake Property

Premier Lake Property • Sulphur
580-622-6125 • www.premierlakeproperty.com

Premier Lake Property is the doorway to a relaxing, yet energizing getaway. Have meetings, retreats or family vacations at any of the Premier lakefront homes. Each cabin is themed and provides all the amenities of home.

The properties are nestled in the serene Arbuckle Mountain area of Southern Oklahoma. Lake Arbuckle, one of Oklahoma's most pristine lakes, is only a few minutes away. The Chickasaw National Recreation Area, Turner Falls Park and Arbuckle Wilderness Exotic Animal Park are all less than 10 minutes away.

EAT

Venison Sloppy Joe Mix

4 pounds ground venison
  with no fat added
3 cups chopped onions
1½ cups chopped bell peppers
2 cups bacon fat
2 cups ketchup

1 can tomato paste (small)
2 tablespoons garlic powder
1 tablespoon salt
¾ teaspoon pepper
1 tablespoon sugar
2½ cups water

Cook venison and onions until brown. Pour off excess fat. Add all other ingredients; mix thoroughly. Bring to a boil and simmer 5 minutes. Pack into clean Mason pint jars, leaving 1-inch head space. Adjust lids. Process at 15 pounds pressure for 75 minutes, or 10 pounds pressure for 110 minutes. Makes 8 pints. May also be frozen in pint-size freezer containers. To serve, heat and serve over your favorite bun or bread.

Deer Festival & Outdoor Show

Deer Festival & Outdoor Show

First Weekend of October

Antlers Fairgrounds • Antlers
580-298-9933 • www.wildlifeheritagecenter.org

The Deer Festival has various displays of hunting and fishing activities with experts available to answer questions or to just talk with. There are approximately 60 to 70 vendors at the Deer Festival to accommodate the visitors. Many of the vendors have raffles for rifles, feeders, etc. The Deer Capital Tourism Association is the organization that produces this festival and raffles off a hunting cabin each year. Events at the Deer Festival include wildlife photo contest, chainsaw carving, camp chili cook-off and cutest kids in camo contest. There is live entertainment on an outdoor stage for the majority of the Festival. The Deer Capital Tourism Association also sponsors the Wildlife Heritage Center Museum. The Wildlife Center Museum is open during the Festival for visitors to see many mounted displays of wildlife, most of which are native to Oklahoma. There is a "hands on" table for the kids to explore. There are live White Tail deer that can be hand fed also. Admission is free to both the Deer Festival and the Wildlife Heritage Center Museum.

Venison Roast

1 venison roast
1 package dry onion soup
  mix
1 teaspoon garlic powder

1 cup sherry wine
1 tablespoon sugar
Sage to taste

Wash venison roast thoroughly. Preheat oven to 425° then reduce heat to 350°. Place roast on a large piece of heavy duty aluminum foil. Sprinkle ½ to entire package dry onion soup mix over meat. Wrap venison in the foil and seal edges tightly. Place in a baking pan and roast 2 to 2½ hours or until tender. Remove roast to a plate. Pour off any fat from juices. To pan juices, add red wine, sugar and sage. Thicken with flour or cornstarch to make a gravy. (Tip: use cornstarch if you want a lighter gravy.)

Deer Festival & Outdoor Show

Scrumptious Sirloin Steaks

2 top-sirloin steaks
4 garlic cloves, pressed
¼ cup olive oil
2 teaspoons dried basil

2 teaspoons dried oregano
2 teaspoons dried parsley
1 teaspoon dried rosemary
Salt and pepper

In a small bowl, mix together garlic, olive oil, basil, oregano, parsley and rosemary. Sprinkle steaks with salt and pepper, then rub with garlic mixture. Cover and chill steaks at least 2 hours. Before cooking, sprinkle with a bit more salt. Place steaks on grill and close lid. Cook over high heat till desired doneness.

Smoky Beef Tenderloin and Big Red Steak Wine

Line a large baking dish with Saran Wrap overlapping the sides (if it will fit in a plastic bag, even better). Place tenderloin in the middle of wrap. Cover tenderloin with a generous dose of Lea and Perrins Worcestershire Sauce. Fold plastic wrap over tenderloin so that sauce is contained and meat is covered. Marinate at least 2 hours at room temperature. Turn meat occasionally, to be sure all surfaces have been in contact with sauce.

About 3 hours before desired serving time, start a large pile of charcoal. When charcoal is fully engaged and surface is covered with grey embers, spread charcoal out. Place tenderloin on grill and let it sear 3 to 5 minutes on each side. Move tenderloin to cool side of grill or smoking side of cooker. Be sure meat is not directly over fire. Add small logs of freshly cut wood to top of charcoal to begin smoking process. I like to use black jack oak but feel free to experiment with other species. Pour remaining marinade over tenderloin and shake a generous amount of garlic pepper on meat. On a smoker that reaches 300° in the smoking chamber, it will take about 1½ to 2 hours to reach medium rare. This of course depends on size of tenderloin and heat. If meat is on cool side of a covered grill, you will probably want to turn meat every 20 to 30 minutes, and it will be ready in less time. Allow tenderloin to rest about 10 minutes before cutting.

I like to have thick slices of meat with a béarnaise sauce. It can also be thinly sliced.

When pairing food and wine, you want to have equal intensities.

from Tom's lovely Mother, June
Redbud Ridge Vineyard & Winery

Grilled Steaks on the Lake

½ cup olive oil
¼ cup Worcestershire sauce
6 tablespoons soy sauce
¼ cup minced garlic
½ medium onion, chopped
2 tablespoons sea salt

1 tablespoon freshly ground pepper
3 tablespoons steak seasoning
3 tablespoons A-1 steak sauce
3 tablespoons liquid smoke
4 (10-ounce) rib-eye steaks

Combine olive oil, Worcestershire sauce, soy sauce, garlic, onion, salt, pepper, steak seasoning, steak sauce and liquid smoke in the container of a food processor or blender. Process until well blended. Prick steaks on both sides with a fork, and place in a shallow container with a lid. Pour marinade over steaks, cover, and refrigerate at least 3 hours, or overnight. Preheat an outdoor grill for medium heat. Remove steaks from marinade, and discard marinade. Lightly oil grilling surface, and place steaks on the grill. Cover and grill steaks about 10 minutes on each side, or cooked to your desire.

Lake Murray Bed & Berth

Lake Murray Bed & Berth

Lake Murray State Park • Ardmore
580-223-0088 • www.oklahomabedandberth.com

Imagine watching the sunrise from a private balcony or the sunset from a deck. The Floating Vacation Villas hold the essence of what Lake Murray Bed and Berth offers—living rooms with panoramic views of the lake and its wooded coves, white pine vaulted ceilings, cozy sleeping lofts, and sweeping verandas and balconies to watch the sunset or the sunrise. A kitchen, full baths with showers, and master bedrooms with spacious closets offer all the amenities of home. The Villas and Gazebo are in a gated area at Tranquility Point, just three miles off of Interstate 35 at Exit 24. The Atrium, Cottage, and Dockaminium Villas are located on the peninsula north of Lake Murray Lodge, also off of Interstate 35 at Exit 24. There are three restaurants, a golf course, and an airport one mile away. Boats, jet skis, and any other watercraft can be moored at each Villa. Take a look around their website for more information about the luxurious Lake Murray Floating Vacation Villas. There is also information about hiking, house boating, biking, camping, fishing, skiing, and the many other activities offered.

Grilled Rib-Eye

1 (16-ounce) Certified Angus Beef Rib-Eye steak

Rub with salt, pepper and granulated garlic. Let sit at room temperature for 20 minutes. Cook over hot fire 4 minutes per side for medium doneness.

Oklahoma Championship Steak Cook-Off

Oklahoma Championship Steak Cook-Off

August

Downtown Tulsa
918.582.4128 extension 103
www.oksteakcookoff.com

A cloud of fragrant smoke covers downtown Tulsa like a blanket. The smell of sizzling beef rides on the summer breeze. There is music in the air. It's August, it's downtown, it's the Oklahoma Championship Steak Cook-off.

The cook-off features 50 + teams competing to see who can cook the best steak in Oklahoma.

The day starts out with the teams preparing appetizers. There is seafood and sausage, duck and doughnuts, and much more, all covered in the price of admission.

In addition, a huge classic car show, vendors, and other activities abound.

Once the competition steaks have been turned in to the judging table the attention turns to the main event of the afternoon. The largest steak dinner ever held in Oklahoma.

The Oklahoma Championship Steak Cook-off is the largest event of its kind in the southwest and one of the fastest growing festivals in Oklahoma. The OCSC is unique in the fact that 100% of the proceeds from this event are earmarked to assist the needy of Tulsa. In the past two years the organizers have donated more than $30,000 to groups like the Iron Gate, Community Food Bank and Habitat for Humanity.

Sid's Onion Burger

For these "addictively" tasty burgers, ground beef is pressed onto the griddle with paper-thin slices of onion and seared until crisp around the edges.

4 tablespoons canola oil
1 pound ground beef, gently formed into 6 balls
2 medium yellow onions, very thinly sliced and divided into 6 equal
   portions
Kosher salt to taste
6 slices American cheese
6 hamburger buns, toasted

Working in 2 batches, heat 2 tablespoons oil in a 12-inch cast-iron skillet over medium-high heat. Add 3 beef balls and, using the back of a spatula, press down on them until very thin; cook 1 minute. Top each patty with a portion of the onions; season with salt. Press onions into the meat and cook 1 minute more. Flip burgers; flatten with spatula. Place a cheese slice on each patty and let melt while onions and meat brown. Serve on buns.

Sid's Diner
El Reno Convention & Visitors Bureau

El Reno, Oklahoma

El Reno Convention & Visitors Bureau

110 South Bickford Avenue • El Reno
405-262-8687 or 888-535-7366
www.elrenotourism.com

Located at the intersection of historic Route 66 and the Chisholm Trail is El Reno. Named after Civil War hero General Jesse L. Reno, the city is a festival town and boasts many heritage celebrations, historic properties and the only rail based trolley in the state.

Dubbed "The Heritage Express", the trolley is kept on the grounds of the Canadian County Historical Museum and travels through the downtown area. One of the many stops along the way is the Centre Theatre. An architectural and artistic centerpiece for the City of El Reno, the Centre Theatre draws audiences from the surrounding communities, across the state and around the nation.

Visit the website to learn more about other El Reno attractions. Fort Reno, the Canadian County Historical Museum, and Lake El Reno are just a couple of examples of what's waiting at America's Crossroad.

Boeuf en Daube

2 pounds steak (round or sirloin), cubed
2 tablespoons butter
¼ cup cognac
½ pound mushrooms, sliced
20 olives, sliced
1 can tomato paste
3 tablespoons flour
1½ cups seasoned stock (canned bouillon or consommé)
¾ cups red wine
1 teaspoon herb bouquet
2 tablespoons red currant jelly
Salt and fresh ground pepper to taste

Brown steak quickly in butter. Pour cognac over beef and ignite. When flames die, remove beef. Combine mushrooms and olives with beef and cook 5 minutes. Add remaining ingredients. Simmer 1 hour (minimum) or until beef is tender. This improves with age, like wine and winemakers, so you can make ahead and reheat for dinner or party. Serve with wild rice and black rye bread.

from Tom's lovely Mother, June
Redbud Ridge Vineyard & Winery

Tater Tot Casserole

2 pounds hamburger meat
1 can cream of mushroom soup
1 can cream of chicken soup
1 regular size bag frozen tater tots

Preheat oven to 375°. Brown hamburger in a skillet and drain. Stir in both cans of soup (no water). Pour into casserole dish and top with tater tots. Bake until bubbly and tater tots are brown.

Pearl Morrow
The Dehydrator

Beef and Rice Casserole

1 pound sausage or hamburger
1 cup uncooked rice
1 cup chopped onion
3 cups diced celery
2 cans cream of mushroom soup

Brown meat and drain well. Cook rice with onions and celery according to directions. When rice is tender, stir in soup and hamburger. Pour into 2 casserole dishes and bake 45 minutes in a 350° oven.

Karolyn Anders
Holiday in the Park

Indian Tacos

5 cups flour
5 teaspoons baking powder
½ teaspoon salt
Vegetable oil
1 large can refried beans
1 pound ground beef, browned
½ head lettuce, shredded

2 large tomatoes, chopped fine
1 large onion, chopped fine
1 pound grated sharp Cheddar
 cheese
Salt and pepper to taste
Salsa to taste, optional

Combine flour, baking powder and salt. Add water in small amounts just until you get a workable dough. Make into large ball. Let stand 20 minutes. Get oil real hot (donut hot). Take golf-ball-size pinches off. Roll on floured surface by hand. Play with dough ball until large saucer size (or use rolling pin). Drop into hot oil and fry until golden brown. Drain on paper towels. Top each fry bread with refried beans, ground beef, lettuce, tomatoes, onions and cheese. Salt and pepper to taste. Top with salsa if desired.

LEFTOVER BREAD FOR BREAKFAST: Reheat in microwave. Sprinkle with cinnamon/sugar combination or top with butter and honey.

Elk City Fall Festival

Elk City Fall Festival
Third Weekend of November

Elk City Convention Center
1016 East Airport Industrial Road
Elk City

Sponsored by the Elk City Chamber of Commerce
800-280-0207 or 580-225.0207 • www.visitelkcity.com

Always the third weekend of November, the Annual Elk City Fall Festival boasts the largest arts and crafts show in western Oklahoma. For almost 40 years, hundreds of crafters and artists from all over the Midwest participate in this event in order to showcase their unique gifts, products and home décor. Area high school students display their art work for judging and the Kid's Corner features arts and craft projects designed just for the little kids. During this annual

event, food concessions offer up delectable treats for every appetite. There is always free parking and free admission at the Annual Elk City Fall Festival. When visiting the Annual Fall Festival visitors will also enjoy a stop at Elk City's National Route 66 Museum Complex which features the Old Town Museum, Transportation Museum, Farm and Ranch Museum, and the Blacksmith Museum.

Corpus Christi-Style Enchiladas

1 pound ground beef
1 large onion, minced
3 tablespoons chili powder, divided
Salt and pepper
2 cups cubed Velveeta cheese
3 tablespoons flour
1½ cups water
3 tablespoons tomato sauce or ketchup
16 to 18 tortillas
½ cup grated Cheddar or Jack cheese, optional

Brown ground beef in skillet, stirring constantly to keep separated. Add onion, cook until transparent. Stir in 2 tablespoons chili powder, salt and pepper to taste and Velveeta cheese. Cover and set aside. Mix flour and water together to make a smooth paste. Combine flour mixture, remaining 1 tablespoon chili powder and tomato sauce in a saucepan. Season to taste with salt and pepper; heat thoroughly. Sauce should be consistency of medium white sauce. Add additional water or flour as needed. Dip each tortilla in sauce. Fill with 1 heaping tablespoon beef mixture; roll tightly. Repeat until all are prepared; stack if necessary to get all in casserole. Pour remaining sauce over top. Bake at 350° for 10 to 15 minutes or until heated through. Garnish with additional ½ cup grated cheese, if desired. Yield 5 to 6 servings. Purchased enchilada sauce can be substituted in place of the sauce, if desired.

Sondra Martin
Bedstead Retreat

Enchilada Casserole

2 pounds ground beef
½ clove garlic, minced
1 teaspoon salt
½ teaspoon pepper
1 large onion, chopped

1 small can green chiles, chopped
1 large can green enchilada sauce
1 pound grated sharp Cheddar
   cheese
Flour tortillas

Preheat oven to 350°. Brown meat with garlic, salt, pepper and onion. Drain. Add green chiles and enchilada sauce; mix well. Heat 2 or 3 tortillas at a time in a microwave. Spoon about 2 or 3 tablespoons meat mixture down center of each tortilla and roll up. Lay in a greased 9x13-inch baking dish until dish is full. Spoon a thin layer of the enchilada meat over all and top with cheese. Bake 20 minutes.

Jane Apple
Hitching Post Bed & Breakfast

Beef Mexican Casserole

1 pound ground beef
1 (4-ounce) can green chiles
1 (10-ounce) can enchilada sauce
½ cup milk or cream
1 (10-ounce) can cream of
   mushroom soup

½ cup salsa
Corn tortillas (as many or as few
   as you like)
16 ounces shredded mild Cheddar
   cheese

Preheat oven to 375°. Brown and drain ground beef. Add all ingredients, except cheese and tortillas. In a 9x13-inch dish layer tortillas, ½ ground beef mixture, tortillas and remaining mixture. Top with cheese and bake until bubbly and cheese is melted.

Anita Peddycoart
The Dehydrator

Game Day Casserole

1 (7-ounce) package elbow
  macaroni
1 pound ground beef
1 egg, beaten
1 onion, diced
½ green bell pepper, diced

Salt and pepper to taste
2 cans cream of mushroom soup
1¼ cups water
1 (16-ounce) carton sour cream
1 can green peas, drained

Preheat oven to 350°. Cook macaroni according to package directions. Mix ground beef, egg, onion and green pepper in a medium bowl. Season with salt and pepper. Make into meatballs and brown in a skillet, draining off fat. Remove meatballs and set aside. Combine cream of mushroom, water, sour cream and cooked macaroni in a large bowl and blend well. Add peas and meatballs, mixing thoroughly. Grease a large casserole dish and pour in meatball mixture. Cover tightly and bake 35 minutes.

Libertyfest

USA Today declared LibertyFest in Edmond as one of the top ten places to be in America on July 4th. This week long event celebrates the birthday of this great nation and Oklahoma's heritage. Over 150,000 people come to honor America's independence at this fun-filled event.

Visit online at www.libertyfest.org to learn dates, location and times.

UCO Endeavor Games

June

University of Central Oklahoma • Edmond
405-974-3160 • www.ucoendeavorgames.com

The University of Central Oklahoma is proud to present the UCO Endeavor Games, a nationally recognized competition that allows all athletes with physical disabilities to participate in a multi-sport event. The games also provide training clinics for aspiring athletes.

The UCO Endeavor games hosts eleven sport competitions annually each June. Athletes are encouraged to participate in as many sports as possible, without conflicts in time. Indoor/outdoor archery, cycling, powerlifting, sitting volleyball, shooting, swimming, table tennis, track & field and wheelchair basketball 3-on-3 (juniors and adults).

All activities are held in Edmond at the University of Central Oklahoma, Edmond North High School, or the Lake Arcadia Outdoor Adventure Recreation Center.

The UCO Endeavor Games is supported or sanctioned by U.S. Paralympics, Disabled Sports USA, USA Track and Field, Wheelchair Sports USA, and USA Archery.

Kim and Bob's Hot Coffee Steak

Ribeye steak
Fresh ground coffee
Salt and pepper

Jalapeños, chopped
Lard or shortening
Brewed, hot coffee

Coat steaks well with mixture of fresh ground coffee, salt and pepper and jalapeños. Melt 2 to 3 tablespoons lard in Dutch oven over hot coals. Add steak and sear on all sides. Remove half the coals to use on top of lid. Pour in enough hot coffee to cover bottom of oven. Put on lid and add coals to top. Add additional hot coffee, as needed. Cook to preferred doneness (5 to 10 minutes for medium rare). Let stand 5 minutes before serving.

Running M Ranch, El Reno, Oklahoma
Chuck Wagon Gathering & Children's Cowboy Festival

Western Heritage Museum

Chuck Wagon Gathering & Children's Cowboy Festival

Memorial Day Weekend

Held at the National Cowboy Museum
1700 NE 63rd Street
Oklahoma City
405-478-2250
www.nationalcowboymuseum.org

Come to Oklahoma City, home of the National Cowboy & Western Heritage Museum®. This first-class Museum attracts visitors from around the world. Known for more than three decades as the National Cowboy Hall of Fame, the Museum sports a new name more reflective of its tremendous collection of

art, objects and research materials helpful in preserving and interpreting the Cowboy's history of the American West.

Held annually at the museum is the Chuck Wagon Gathering & Children's Cowboy Festival. Two days of mouth-watering campfire cooked foods, children's educational hands-on activities, Western stage entertainment and stagecoach and pony rides await visitors to the Museum's largest outdoor event.

Jerky

2 pounds round steak
Salt and pepper to taste
Hickory smoked salt to taste
¼ teaspoon garlic salt
Sugar to taste

Trim fat from round steak. Place meat in freezer 1 to 2 hours until frosty so it is easier to cut. Slice into thin strips. Place in shallow baking pan or dish in layers. Sprinkle each layer with seasonings. Cover with foil. Place weight at the top of foil and refrigerate overnight. Drain. Place in shallow baking pan. Bake at 250° for 3 to 5 hours depending on thickness of meat.

Harn Homestead & 1889ers Museum

Ranch Hand Beef Jerky

5 pounds lean beef, trimmed and
   cut ¼-inch thick across the grain
1 cup Worcestershire sauce
½ cup soy sauce
2 teaspoons onion powder
2 teaspoons garlic powder
2 teaspoons cayenne pepper
   powder
¼ cup coarse ground black pepper

Combine all ingredients in a bowl. Add more of either liquid if necessary to cover meat. Cover and refrigerate 24 to 48 hours. Remove from refrigerator, drain and place on dehydrator racks. Sprinkle with additional black pepper. Do not let pieces touch each other. Follow dehydrator instructions. Oven option: Place on oven racks with a drip pan at the bottom of the oven. Cook at 150° for approximately 10 hours.

Buffalo Creek Guest Ranch

Schnitzel with Mushrooms in Cream Sauce

4 ounces beef tenderloin
Pinch salt, white pepper, paprika
  and Knorr Meat Aromat
  Seasoning
4 ounces heavy cream
1 teaspoon Maggi seasoning liquid

4 ounces fresh, sautéed mushrooms
  (a jar of cooked mushrooms is
  acceptable)
1 tablespoon cornstarch
½ cup water

Grill or sauté medallions of beef tenderloin in pan. Season with spices. When meat is at desired doneness remove from pan and keep warm. Pour cream in pan, add Maggi seasoning liquid and stir until full boil. Add mushrooms. Mix cornstarch and water and add slowly to boiling mushroom sauce, just enough to thicken to desired creamy texture. Place medallions on center plate and pour sauce to cover meat. Garnish with parsley and serve with red cabbage and choice of starch. Serve a chilled Sauvignon Blanc or a Rheingau Riesling Kabinett with this entrée.

Mike Turek
Old Germany Restaurant

Old Germany Restaurant

On March 1, 1976 with little left to lose but our last $300, my family opened Old Germany Restaurant on March 1, 1976 with only one German dish – Wiener Schnitzel. Over the years patrons discovered what German food is all about, and today the menu offers a wide array of 100% German cuisine. The website is www.oldgermany.com, and there you will find the complete menu, learn a bit of history, see some photos and learn about the various events the restaurant hosts each year.

—Mike Turek

German-Style Meatballs

1 pound ground beef
1 pound ground pork
3 small onions, chopped
6 tablespoons oil, divided
8 tablespoons breadcrumbs or
  2 slices white bread
½ cup milk
2 teaspoons basil
2 teaspoons salt
2 teaspoons pepper
2 teaspoons flour

Mix ground meats together in a mixing bowl. Sauté onions in 1 tablespoon oil until transparent; add to meat mixture. In a separate bowl, stir together breadcrumbs and milk. Add to meat mixture. Add basil, salt, pepper, flour and mix well. Dampen hands and form meat mixture into meatballs or flat patties. Fry on both sides in remaining 5 tablespoons oil until golden brown.

Choctaw Oktoberfest

Choctaw Oktoberfest

**Weekend before and
Week after Labor Day**

Choctaw Creek Park on Harper Road
Choctaw
405-390-8647
www.oldgermany.com

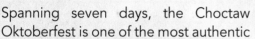

Spanning seven days, the Choctaw Oktoberfest is one of the most authentic festivals of Oklahoma. Sponsored by the city of Choctaw, the Choctaw Chamber, Old Germany Restaurant and many area businesses, the festival's center is the pavilion in beautiful Choctaw Creek Park, located on Harper Street, ½ mile south of NE 23rd Street in Choctaw.

The annual Oktoberfest celebration has become a favorite destination for visitors from a multi-state area seeking homemade German food, genuine German beers, wine, and German music. 30,000 square feet of tents and pavilion provide a real German-Fest atmosphere.

There are 30 original German Draught Beers and International Wines to complement the menu. Visitors can feast on Schweinshaxen (ham hocks), Grilled Chicken, Rippchen (smoked pork chops) and a variety of bratwurst and Schnitzel sandwiches, Red Cabbage, Sauerkraut, German Potato Salad and Apple Strudel—all homemade in the Old Germany Festival Kitchen!

In addition to food and drink, there is live entertainment, complete with authentic German dance.

Marinated Pork Tenderloin

1 cup red raspberry preserves
¼ cup jalapeño jelly
½ cup liquid smoke
Greek seasoning and seasoning salt to taste
2 small pork tenderloins

Mix everything but pork together in a large storage bag. Close bag and knead to combine ingredients. Add pork tenderloin and let it marinate overnight. Grill to your liking and enjoy!

Jimmy Tramel, Mayor
Dam J.A.M.

Dam J.A.M.

Saturday following Labor Day

Whitaker Park
Pryor
918-825-0157
www.pryorchamber.com

DAM J.A.M. is Oklahoma's most scenic one-day bicycle tour and fabulous fall family event featuring fun rides of 30, 55, 71, or 101 miles!

Located in the heart of Oklahoma's Green Country within beautiful Mayes and Delaware Counties, the tour starts and finishes in Pryor's Whitaker Park.

The Pryor community is within riding distance of more than 2,500 miles of lake shoreline in the gentle foothills of the Ozark Mountains.

Participants will experience lush countryside, well-paved, shady rural roads, DAM J.A.M.'s world-famous festive rest stops, and some of the best support of any bicycle ride... anywhere.

Pork Roast

1 (3-pound) pork roast
Salt and pepper
Garlic powder
1 large onion, thickly sliced
1 tablespoon caraway seeds
2 cups water (approximate)

Sprinkle salt, pepper and garlic powder over pork. Place meat in a Dutch oven and layer onions and caraway on top. Add enough water for ¼ of the meat to sit in. Cover and place in preheated 400° oven. Bake 10 minutes. Turn temperature down to 350° and bake 1½ hours (approximately 30 minutes per pound). After baking time, if meat needs a darker color, remove lid and continue baking an additional 10 to 15 minutes to brown.

This is the Czech Republic's National Dish and is served with gravy, Czech dumplings and cabbage.

Kolache Festival

Crockpot Cranberry "Porkie" Roast

1 boneless rolled pork loin roast
1 (10-ounce) can jellied cranberry
   sauce
¼ cup sugar
½ cup cranberry juice
1 teaspoon dry mustard
¼ teaspoon ground cloves
½ teaspoon nutmeg
Salt and pepper to taste
2 tablespoons cornstarch
2 tablespoons water

Place roast in slow cooker. In medium bowl, mash cranberry sauce; stir in sugar, cranberry juice, mustard, cloves, nutmeg, salt and pepper. Pour over meat. Cover and cook on low for 6 to 8 hours or until meat is tender. Remove roast and keep warm. Skim fat from juices; measure 2 cups of juice, adding water if necessary. Bring to boil. Mix cornstarch and 2 tablespoons water to make a paste. Stir into gravy. Cook and stir until thickened. Season if necessary. Serve with pork.

Courtesy of Santa's Old Broads
Pelican Festival

Peach Habanero Pulled Pork

PULLED PORK:

Pork shoulder

Salt, pepper and garlic powder

Olive oil

4 cups peach nectar

Rub down pork shoulder with salt, pepper and garlic powder. Brown on all sides in skillet with olive oil. Add peach nectar and 3 cups water to crockpot. Cook on high 4 to 4½ hours. (Meat should be falling apart.)

HOT SAUCE:

5 habañero peppers

3 jalapeño peppers

1 large bell pepper

1 cup white vinegar

Slice habañero, jalapeño and bell peppers; grill until they look dried out. Place them in a blender with vinegar. Blend well. If sauce is too thick add more vinegar. Add to barbecue sauce (below) to taste; refrigerate rest for future use.

BARBECUE SAUCE:

3 large peaches

1 cup brown sugar

½ cup rum

¼ cup soy sauce

¼ cup Worcestershire sauce

¼ cup ketchup

2 cloves crushed garlic

1 teaspoon dry mustard

Puréed peaches

Purée peaches in blender. Combine peaches and remaining ingredients in a saucepan. Add pepper sauce to taste for desired heat (a little goes a long way). Heat to boiling then reduce to simmer. Simmer 25 minutes, stirring occasionally. After pork is done, drain then return pork to crockpot. Pull pork apart using 2 forks. Add barbecue sauce and mix well. Pork is good alone but is also great for barbecue sandwiches.

Jeremiah Fletcher

Peach Festival

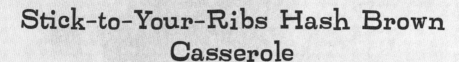

Stick-to-Your-Ribs Hash Brown Casserole

1 pound hot bulk sausage
2 cups shredded Cheddar cheese
1 can cream of chicken soup
1 cup sour cream
1 (8-ounce) container French onion dip
1 cup chopped onion
¼ cup chopped green bell pepper
¼ cup chopped red bell pepper
Salt and pepper to taste
1 (30-ounce) package frozen hash browns, thawed

Preheat oven to 350°. Brown sausage and drain. In a separate bowl, combine cheese, chicken soup, sour cream, French onion dip, onion, bell peppers, salt and pepper. Fold in thawed hash browns and mix well. Spread ½ mixture in a greased 9x13-inch baking dish, top with ½ browned sausage. Repeat a second layer. Bake 1 hour.

Wood Guest Ranch

Wood Guest Ranch

245 E CR 2020 • Boswell
580-566-1300 or 580-317-6970
www.woodsguestranch.com

Saddle-up for a Western adventure! Located in the Clear Boggy River Bottom area of Southeastern Oklahoma is Wood Guest Ranch. Offering Oklahoma Trail riding at its finest, the seasoned and novice outdoorsman will enjoy pristine outdoor setting where the Caddo and Choctaw Indians used to travel and hunt.

In addition to world-class trail rides, Wood Guest Ranch hosts hunting expeditions, family vacation and reunions, and business workshop retreats. They have facilities available for a full range of needs including a covered Pavilion for dining and entertainment, a full arena for rodeos and shows, wash racks and pen rentals for horses and a general store. Come experience the finest Oklahoma Trail Riding in the state.

Located on the Ranch is Hunter Prairie. Hunter Prairie Game Ranch serves as a hunter's paradise. The Clear Boggy River runs through the ranch and provides great river bottom foliage, wooded and marsh areas for a great hunting experience. This part of Wood Guest Ranch provides for your outdoor enjoyment and bird hunting experience.

Succotash

¼ cup olive oil
2 onions, chopped
2 bell peppers, chopped
1 to 2 tablespoons Tony
   Chachere's Creole seasoning
   (or to taste)

1 bag frozen southern-style
   potatoes (square cut)
1 bag frozen corn
1 bag frozen lima beans
2 pounds smoked sausage or
   chicken

Heat oil in skillet. Sauté onions and peppers until onions are clear, season to taste. Add other ingredients and continue to cook until potatoes have browned. Turn often.

Dee Dillow
Country Road BBQ
Roberts Ranch Smokin' Red Dirt BBQ Festival

Roberts Ranch Smokin' Red Dirt BBQ Festival

Third Weekend in April

Cherokee Strip Conference Center
Downtown Enid
Enid Convention & Visitors Bureau
877-999-3643 • 580-548-8194
www.reddirtbbq.com
www.visitenid.org

What started as a backyard barbecue contest in Enid in 2005 gradually took on extra sizzle, transforming downtown into a huge community-wide celebration featuring music, art and entertainment as well as tasty food. Meat roasts and smokes as dozens of competition barbecue teams vie for a Kansas City Barbeque Society officially sanctioned state championship. Festival-goers can put some pork on their fork by participating in the people's choice sampling Friday evening and a noon barbecue lunch on Saturday hosted by the local AMBUCS club. A Friday evening jazz stroll dishes up live music at various downtown venues, and a juried art show includes activities for local youth. A mix of popular street entertainers, like pony rides and magicians, adds to the carnival atmosphere that offers something for everyone against the nostalgic backdrop of Enid's traditional old town square.
— Candace Krebs

Spiced King Prawns

½ cup extra virgin olive oil
8 garlic gloves, minced
1 (heaping) tablespoon ground paprika
1 teaspoon ground cumin
1½ teaspoons ground ginger
½ to ¾ teaspoon cayenne pepper (depending on spice
   preference)
3 pounds large shrimp (shelled and deveined)
¼ teaspoon salt
1 cup coarsely chopped fresh cilantro

Heat olive oil in large skillet. Add garlic, paprika, cumin, ginger and
cayenne. Cook over medium high heat until scents are pronounced (1
to 2 minutes). Add shrimp, stirring continuously; cook 3 to 4 minutes.
Add salt and cilantro and mix well. Yields 8 servings.

Mabee-Gerrer Museum of Art
Shawnee Convention & Visitors Bureau

Citizen Potawatomi Nation
Cultural Heritage Center

Shawnee Convention & Visitors Bureau

131 North Bell • Shawnee
888-404-9633
www.visitshawnee.com

You are cordially invited to "Get Away & Play"! A true treasure to be discovered, Shawnee is located just 35 miles east of Oklahoma City off I-40. The city has unique shopping, delicious dining, wonderful lodging, and truly grand attractions and events. For details and more information visit their site online or follow on twitter @VisitShawneeOK and on facebook VisitShawneeOklahoma.

Scottish Eggs

Submitted by a long time volunteer, these have been served for breakfast on many chilly mornings while setting up the fair.

4 large eggs
1 pound mixed bulk sausage (I use a blend of sage,
   Italian and mild pork sausage)
12 ounces seasoned breadcrumbs

Soft boil eggs. Cool under cold water and peel. Divide sausage into 4 pieces and shape into flat patties. Wrap each egg in 1 patty and make sure there are no bare patches. Roll in breadcrumbs. Place on a baking sheet and bake at 350° for 35 to 40 minutes or until sausage is baked. Cool. Eat hot or cold. (Cannot be frozen.) Makes 4.

Sena Brothers
Medieval Fair

Desserts & Other Sweets

Oatmeal Cake

2 cups water
3 sticks butter
½ cup oatmeal
2 cups flour
1½ cups brown sugar
1½ cups sugar
1 teaspoon cinnamon
1½ teaspoons baking soda
Dash salt
3 eggs

Bring water and butter to a boil. Remove from heat and add oatmeal. Let cool 20 minutes. In large bowl combine flour, brown sugar, sugar, cinnamon, baking soda and salt. Pour cooled oatmeal mixture from saucepan over dry mixture in bowl. Add eggs and mix well. Pour into a greased and floured 9x13-inch pan. Bake at 350° for 30 to 40 minutes.

ICING:

¾ stick melted butter
¼ cup half n' half
1½ cups sifted powdered sugar
2 teaspoons vanilla
Nuts and coconut for garnish (optional)

Mix all ingredients together until creamy. Frost while cake is hot and sprinkle with nuts and coconut.

Noble House Bed & Breakfast and Restaurant

Noble House Bed & Breakfast and Restaurant

112 North Noble • Watonga
580-623-2559 • www.noblehousebb.net

Restaurant hours:
Mon – Sun 5:30 am to 2 pm
For room reservations call 405-201-8887

Enjoy the elegance and the inspiration of the Noble House Bed & Breakfast and Restaurant. Built in 1912 as a boarding house and becoming a hotel 1937, the beautiful Noble House building is listed on the National Registry of Historical Buildings. A fine restaurant is downstairs and five rooms were completed in May of 2004. Named after citizens who contributed greatly to the Watonga community, each room has a TV, a DVD player, and high-speed internet. Breakfast is included and can be served in the restaurant during the morning or served in the upstairs area at a specific time. Call for room reservations or just come to eat.

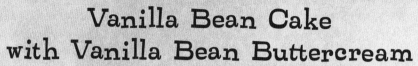

Vanilla Bean Cake
with Vanilla Bean Buttercream

2¼ cups flour
1 tablespoon baking powder
¼ teaspoon salt
8 ounces sweet butter, softened
1¾ cups sugar

1 vanilla bean, split and seeds
  scraped
3 eggs
1¾ cups milk

Sift flour, baking powder and salt. Cream together butter and sugar. Blend in vanilla seeds. Add eggs 1 at a time. Mix after each addition. Alternate adding dry ingredients with milk; blend well but do not overbeat. Divide batter into 2 greased and floured round 8-inch cake pans. Bake in preheated 350° oven until done, about 40 minutes. Cool on rack; remove, fill and frost.

Note: can be made into cupcakes, reduce baking time to 15 to 18 minutes.

BUTTERCREAM:

2 sticks unsalted butter, softened
1 vanilla bean, halved lengthwise
2½ cups powdered sugar (10
  ounces)

Pinch salt
1 teaspoon vanilla extract
2 tablespoons heavy cream

In a standing mixer fitted with whisk attachment, beat butter at medium-high speed until smooth, about 20 seconds. Using a paring knife, scrape seeds from vanilla bean into butter and beat mixture at medium-high speed to combine, about 15 seconds. Add powdered sugar and salt; beat at medium-low speed until most of the sugar is moistened, about 1 minute. Scrape down bowl and beat at medium speed until mixture is fully incorporated, about 30 seconds. Scrape bowl, add vanilla extract and heavy cream. Beat at medium speed until incorporated, about 20 seconds. Increase speed to medium-high and beat until light and fluffy, about 4 minutes, scraping down bowl once or twice.

Bree Carson
Jazz In June

Poppy Seed Cake

½ cup poppy seeds
¾ cup cream
1 cup sugar
½ cup shortening
2 eggs, well beaten

2 cups flour
3 teaspoons baking powder
½ teaspoon salt
1 teaspoon vanilla

Mix poppy seeds and cream in bowl, warm in microwave and let stand for 30 minutes. With electric mixer, cream sugar and shortening until light and fluffy. Add eggs. Sift flour and dry ingredients; add to egg mixture in batches alternating with poppy seed mixture. Add vanilla and beat about 2 minutes. Turn into a greased Bundt pan that has been coated with sugar. Bake at 350° for 30 minutes or until cake pulls away from sides of pan.

Kolache Festival

Pumpkin Pie Cake

4 eggs, slightly beaten
1 (16-ounce) can pumpkin
1½ cups sugar
2 teaspoons pumpkin pie spice
1 teaspoon salt

1 tall can Milnot (canned milk)
1 package yellow cake mix
2 sticks butter, melted
1 cup chopped nuts

Mix together eggs, pumpkin, sugar, spice, salt and Milnot. Pour into 9x13-inch cake pan. Sprinkle cake mix over top. Sprinkle butter over cake mix. Add nuts to the top. Bake at 350° for 1 to 1½ hours or until tester comes out clean. Does not need frosting.

Virginia Scott
Holiday in the Park

Pumpkin Italian Cream Cake

2 cups brown sugar
1 cup sugar
1½ cups butter
1 (15-ounce) can pumpkin
5 eggs
2 teaspoons vanilla
3 cups flour
½ teaspoon baking soda
½ teaspoon baking powder
1 teaspoon salt
1 teaspoon cinnamon
2 teaspoons pumpkin pie spice
½ cup milk
1 cup chopped walnuts or pecans (optional)

Preheat oven to 350°. Mix together brown sugar, sugar and butter. Beat until creamy. When mixture has turned lighter in color, add pumpkin and blend well. Add eggs, 1 at a time, vanilla, flour, baking soda, baking powder, salt, cinnamon and pumpkin pie spice; mix until smooth.. Add milk and nuts. Pour into 3 (9-inch) cake pans. Bake 30 minutes. Ice with cream cheese frosting.

Soda Fountain Eatery

Soda Fountain Eatery

108 West Broadway Street
Anadarko
405-247-3800

Waiting to be discovered in downtown Anadarko is the most unique dining experience in the region. The Soda Fountain Eatery is a 1901 historic drug store building that has been restored to it's original structure. It has it's original 16-foot tin ceiling tiles, a 25-foot soda fountain (circa 1890), brick exposed plaster walls, original pharmacy fixtures and pharmacy memorabilia. It is owned by Philip (pharmacist) and Phyllis (pastry chef) Melton. The Eatery is filled with antique pub tables and chairs purchased in England and the decor transports guests to another era. The menu is always fresh and a feast for the eyes. Phyllis creates about 100 pastries every day, along with 15 sandwich selections, many beautiful salads, a soup of the day and an entrée special. The Eatery is open only for lunch Tuesday through Friday. Call or come early for the special and soup of the day.

Hummingbird Cake

CAKE:

3 cups flour

2 cups sugar

½ teaspoon salt

1 teaspoon baking soda

1 teaspoon cinnamon

3 eggs, lightly beaten

¾ cup oil

1 teaspoon vanilla

2 (8-ounce) cans crushed
  pineapple with juice

1 cup finely chopped pecans

2 cups mashed ripe bananas

Sift flour, sugar, salt, baking soda and cinnamon together in a mixing bowl. Add eggs and oil. Stir with a wooden spoon until moistened. Stir in vanilla, pineapple and pecans. Stir in bananas. Spoon batter into a well-oiled 12-inch Dutch oven. Bake 45 minutes with 9 coals on bottom and 15 coals on top, or until a toothpick inserted in the middle comes out clean and cake has pulled away from sides. Cool in pan 10 minutes. Turn out onto a cooling rack and cool completely. Frost with Pecan Cream Cheese Frosting.

PECAN CREAM CHEESE FROSTING:

8 ounces cream cheese,
  softened

1 teaspoon vanilla

½ cup butter, softened

4 cups powdered sugar

½ cup finely chopped pecans

Combine cream cheese, vanilla and butter; cream until smooth. Add powdered sugar and mix until light and fluffy. Stir in chopped pecans or sprinkle over top of cake.

Terry & Rhonda Cobb
Charlie Adams Day

Charlie Adams Day

2nd Saturday in September

Downtown Newkirk in the Courthouse Square
580-362-2377 • www.charlieadamsday.com

Charlie Adams Day is Newkirk's heritage festival. Held the second Saturday in September, the event is family friendly. Hosted by Newkirk Main Street, it draws folks from miles around with mouth-watering barbecue and delicious Dutch oven desserts. Kay County's beautiful courthouse, in the heart of Newkirk's National Register District, is the backdrop for all the festivities. Entertainment is provided by an Oklahoma Arts Council Grant and begins at 9:00 a.m. and runs until 3:00 p.m. Great music, storytellers, a gunfight re-enactment, dancing girls, flintknapper, blacksmith, basket weaver and lots of children's games as well as arts and crafts fill out the day. Barbecue teams vie for bragging rights and trophies for their great cooking talents. All the entertainment, provided by the Oklahoma Arts Council, is free of charge to the public.

A little background on the esteemed Charlie Adams. Charlie, a pharmacist, settled in Newkirk in 1899 at the ripe age of 24. At about the same time, he patented Good Luck Liniment. Although the liniment label states "for veterinary use only,"

many Newkirk residents can attest to its healing powers on the human animal also. Adams raised and raced trotters and pacers – with his favorite trotter being named Good Luck after the liniment. In 1949 when Charlie was 74 and Good Luck was 16, they won more races nationally than any other trotting team. The liniment is still made and sold in Newkirk today.

Tutti Frutti Cake

1 can fruit cocktail with juice
2 eggs
2 cups flour
1½ cups sugar

2 teaspoons baking soda
1 teaspoon salt
½ cup chopped pecans
½ cup brown sugar

Mix fruit cocktail, eggs, flour, sugar, baking soda and salt together. Pour batter into greased 9x11-inch baking pan. Sprinkle top of batter with chopped pecans and brown sugar. Bake 45 minutes at 325°.

ICING:

1 stick butter
¾ cup sugar

½ cup shredded coconut
½ cup milk

Combine all ingredients together in medium saucepan. Boil 2 minutes, stirring constantly. Let icing cool slightly and pour over cake. (Icing will be really thin.) Serve plain or with fresh whipped cream.

Janet Brown
Sweet-N-Sassy Cafe
Winner of the National Soul Food Cook-Off held each
January in Muskogee
Heritage Days: A Living History Museum

Fun Fact

The state's name is derived from two Choctaw Indian words: "Okla" meaning people and "humma" meaning red. The name was first recorded by the Spanish explorer Coronado.

Key Lime Cake

1 (3-ounce) package lime-flavored
  gelatin
1⅓ cups sugar
2 cups sifted all-purpose flour
½ teaspoon salt
1 teaspoon baking powder
1 teaspoon baking soda
5 large eggs, slightly beaten

1½ cups vegetable oil
¾ cup orange juice
1 tablespoon lemon juice
½ teaspoon vanilla extract
½ cup lime juice (from about
  25 small Key limes or 4 large
  regular limes)
½ cup powdered sugar

Preheat oven to 350°. Grease and flour 3 (9-inch) round cake pans. In large mixing bowl, mix gelatin, sugar, flour, salt, baking powder and baking soda. Stir to mix well. Add eggs, oil, orange juice, lemon juice and vanilla. Divide batter evenly among pans and bake 35 to 40 minutes. Test by lightly touching tops of layers or inserting a toothpick. Cool layers in pans 5 minutes, then turn them out onto racks.

While the layers are still hot, mix lime juice and powdered sugar and pour it over layers on racks. Piercing layers with a fork will allow glaze to soak in better. Allow layers to cool completely as icing is prepared.

CREAM CHEESE ICING:

½ cup butter, room temperature
1 (8-ounce) package cream cheese, room temperature
1 (1-pound) box powdered sugar

Mix butter and cream cheese until creamy. Beat in powdered sugar until mixture is smooth and easy to spread. Spread icing between layers and on top and sides of cake.

Bree Carson
Jazz In June

Banana Cake with Butter Pecan Cream Cheese Icing

1 white cake mix
½ cup vegetable oil
1 cup water

3 large eggs, beaten
3 ripe bananas, mashed (large chunks)

Preheat oven to 350°. Spray 3 round 8-inch cake pans with nonstick spray. Pour cake mix, oil and water into large mixing bowl and add eggs. Beat on medium speed 4 minutes. Add mashed bananas and continue to beat 1 minute on medium speed, until bananas are mixed with some chunks. Pour into prepared pans and bake on center rack. Cake is done when center springs back when touched. Let cool 5 minutes, turn out onto cooling rack. Refrigerate until cold.

BUTTER PECAN CREAM CHEESE ICING:

1½ cups pecans
1 cup brown sugar
⅓ cup butter
1 (8-ounce) package cream cheese, softened

2 tablespoons milk or cream
1½ teaspoons vanilla
1 pound powdered sugar

Combine pecans, brown sugar and butter in a saucepan. Cook over medium heat until pecans are toasted. Cool in refrigerator until cold. In a separate bowl, beat cream cheese until smooth. Add milk and vanilla; beat until blended. Gradually add powdered sugar; beat until creamy. Add cold butter pecan mixture and mix on low until blended. If icing is too thick, add a few drops of cream or milk. If too thin, add more powdered sugar.

Islia Barnes
Cedar Canyon Lodge & Stables Cantina

Cedar Canyon Lodge & Stables Cantina

216872 State Highway 50A • Freedom
6 Miles South of Freedom, at entrance of Alabaster Caverns State Park
580-621-3258 • www.cedarcanyonlodge.net

Seasonal Hours:
April 1st – October 31st
Mon-Fri 11 am to 9 pm • Sat 9 am to 9 pm • Sun 9 am to 6 pm

November 1st – March 31st
Mon-Thurs 11 am to 8 pm • Sat 9 am to 9 pm • Sun 9 am to 6 pm

Cedar Canyon Lodge & Stables Cantina is a great location to enjoy an adventurous weekend with the family; a beautiful scenic locale for a rehearsal dinner, wedding or reception; holiday and birthday parties; or any other excuse to get away from the hustle of life and just relax and take in the view. Visitors can have a blast at the 3D archery range, and enjoy dinner and drinks at the full restaurant and bar.

The Lodge offers six spacious guest rooms—5 with two queen beds and 1 with a King bed—in a 7000 square foot layout. It features pine log exterior, hand hewn beams which support the cathedral ceilings with interior rooms being of pine and cedar. Rooms are decorated with western furnishings and artwork. Covered porches on the North and South side of the lodge provide comfortable areas where guests can observe abundant wildlife, a variety of birds, canyons and beautiful sunrises and sunsets. They are open year round.

Apple Nut Cake

3 sticks butter or margarine
2 eggs
1 cup evaporated milk (for bread pudding type texture,
 use 1 can evaporated milk)
2 cups flour
2½ cups sugar, divided
2 teaspoons baking powder
5 big apples, peeled and sliced
200 grams chopped nuts (1½ to 2 cups)
2 tablespoons cinnamon
Caramel syrup, optional

Melt butter and let it cool completely. In large bowl, beat butter with eggs and evaporated milk. Then add flour, 1½ cups sugar and baking powder and continue to beat until fully incorporated. Place apples on bottom of a seasoned or prepared 12-inch Dutch oven (or 9x13-inch baking dish). Combine nuts, 1 cup sugar and cinnamon; put half of this mixture over apples. Top with flour mixture then with remaining nut mixture. Bake at 350° in conventional oven till top is golden brown or in Dutch oven with coals (3x above 1x below). Serve warm. Add caramel syrup over top for added flavor

Leigh Ann Matthews
4M Chuck Wagon, Muskogee, OK
Heritage Days: A Living History Festival

Anita's Gooey Cake

2 cups self-rising flour
2½ cups milk, divided
3 cups sugar, divided

2 eggs
1½ teaspoons vanilla , divided
2 sticks butter, divided

Preheat oven to 350°. Grease and flour a 9x13-inch cake pan. Cream together flour, 1½ cups milk, 2 cups sugar, eggs, 1 teaspoon vanilla and 1 stick butter. Pour batter into pan and bake 1 hour. After cake is done, combine remaining 1 cup milk, 1 cup sugar, 1 stick butter, and ½ teaspoon vanilla in a saucepan and bring to a boil. Pour over cake.

Joyce Newkirk
The Dehydrator

Almond Joy Cake

1 chocolate cake mix (with pudding) plus ingredients to prepare per directions
1 (12-ounce) can evaporated milk, divided
2½ cups sugar, divided

24 large marshmallows
14 ounces coconut
½ cup margarine
1 (12-ounce) package chocolate chips
1 cup almonds

Mix and bake cake according to package directions in a 9x13-inch pan. Combine 1 cup evaporated milk, 1 cup sugar, and 24 marshmallows in a saucepan and cook until all is melted. Remove from heat and add coconut. Pour over warm cake. Combine remaining 1½ cups sugar, ½ cup evaporated milk and margarine in a saucepan. Bring to a boil, stirring continuously. Remove from heat and add chocolate chips, stirring until melted. Spoon over cake. Top with nuts. Refrigerate 2 to 4 hours before serving.

Linda Osburn
Sequoyah Fest & Made in Oklahoma Festival

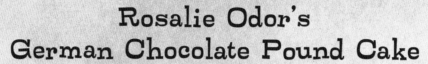

Rosalie Odor's
German Chocolate Pound Cake

Rosalie Odor is the wife of Ralph K. Odor. His dad built the barn in 1898. This recipe was submitted by Rosalie Odor's grandson, Don Morris. "My grandmother used to make this cake and wrap it in wax paper and tin foil and send it to me when I was in college. It seems to get better as it ages. All the guys in my dorm would watch for packages from my grandmother and make sure they were around to get a bite of her cake."

1 bar Baker's German Sweet
  Chocolate
2 cups sugar
1 cup butter, softened
4 eggs

2 teaspoons vanilla
1 cup buttermilk
3 cups sifted all-purpose flour
1 teaspoon salt
½ teaspoon baking soda

Partially melt chocolate over hot water. Remove and stir rapidly until melted. Cream sugar and butter; add eggs, vanilla and buttermilk. Sift together flour, salt and baking soda. Add to mixture and mix well. Blend in melted chocolate until thoroughly mixed. Pour into a greased and floured Bundt pan. Bake in a slow oven at 325° for about an hour and 20 minutes, or until a toothpick inserted comes out clean. Let cake cool 10 minutes. Remove from pan and place under a tightly fitted cover until thoroughly cooled.

GERMAN SWEET CHOCOLATE GLAZE:

1 bar Baker's German Sweet
  Chocolate
1 tablespoon butter
¼ cup water

1 cup powdered sugar
Pinch salt
½ teaspoon vanilla

Melt chocolate and butter in ¼ cup water over low heat. Mix in powdered sugar, salt and vanilla. Glaze should be consistency of honey, it can be thinned by adding a small amount of hot water. Pour over top of cake allowing it to drip over sides evenly. Let cool. If you like, you can dust the cake with powdered sugar instead of using the glaze.

Don Morris
Arcadia Round Barn

Sopapilla Cheesecake

2 cans crescent rolls
2 (8-ounce) packages cream
  cheese
1½ cups sugar, divided

1 teaspoon vanilla
1 stick butter
1 teaspoon cinnamon

Preheat oven to 350°. Press 1 can crescent rolls into bottom of 9x13-inch pan to make crust. Mix cream cheese, 1 cup sugar and vanilla until creamy. Spread over crescent rolls. Cover with second can of crescent rolls. Melt butter, stir in remaining sugar and cinnamon and pour over top of rolls. Bake 30 minutes.

Kim Burge
The Dehydrator

Sopapillas

2 cups flour
2 teaspoons baking powder
1 teaspoon salt

1 teaspoon sugar
1 tablespoon shortening
Warm water

Mix together flour, baking powder, salt and sugar. Cut shortening into flour and mix, adding warm water to make medium soft dough. Put dough in a bowl, cover, and let stand 30 minutes. Roll dough on floured board until ⅛-inch thick. Cut into triangles and deep fry until golden brown. Makes 2 dozen.

Jane Apple
Hitching Post Bed & Breakfast

"Headin' to Market"
statue by Harold Holden

Coconut Cream Pie

¾ cup sugar
3 tablespoons cornstarch
¼ teaspoon salt
2 cups milk
3 egg yolks
2 tablespoons butter
1 teaspoon vanilla
1 cup coconut
1 (9-inch) pastry shell, baked
1 (8-ounce) carton whipped topping

Combine sugar, cornstarch and salt in a medium saucepan; gradually stir in milk. Cook over medium heat, stirring constantly, until thickened. Beat egg yolks in small bowl. Add small amount of hot mixture to egg yolks, beating well. Stir egg mixture into hot mixture. Cook and stir over medium heat 2 minutes. Remove from heat, stir in butter, vanilla and coconut. Spoon mixture into shell. Bake at 350° for 10 minutes. Cool; top with whipped topping. Sprinkle additional coconut on top.

Historic Stockyards City
"Centennial Cookbook" (2010)

Historic Stockyards City

1305 South Agnew
Oklahoma City
405-235-7267
www.stockyardscity.org

One of the oldest and most well preserved historic districts in Oklahoma City, Historic Stockyards City offers Oklahoma hospitality to national and international visitors in search of that authentic western spirit.

Impossible Coconut Pie

1 cup grated coconut
3 eggs, beaten
4 tablespoons butter
½ cup flour
½ teaspoon baking powder
1 cup sugar

¼ teaspoon salt
1 teaspoon vanilla
1 teaspoon grated lemon
2 cups milk
3 tablespoons coconut rum
  (optional)

Combine all ingredients and pour into a buttered pie pan and bake at 350° for 1 hour.

Virginia Scott
Holiday in the Park

Coconut-Caramel Pie

¼ cup butter
1 (7-ounce) package coconut
½ cup chopped pecans
1 (8-ounce) package cream cheese, softened
1 (14-ounce) can sweetened condensed milk
1 (16-ounce) container Cool Whip, thawed
2 graham cracker crusts
1 (12-ounce) jar caramel ice cream topping

Melt butter in large skillet. Add coconut and pecans; cook until golden, stirring constantly. Set aside. Combine cream cheese and sweetened condensed milk. Beat until smooth. Fold in Cool Whip. Layer ¼ cream cheese mixture in the bottom of each crust. Drizzle ¼ of the caramel over each pie, sprinkle ¼ coconut pecan mixture over each pie. Repeat layers with remaining ingredients. Cover and freeze until firm. Let frozen pie stand at room temperature 5 minutes before serving.

Bill Hoag
Arcadia Round Barn

Peach Pie Extraordinaire

FILLING:

12 ounces cream cheese, softened
1¼ cups sugar, divided
3 eggs

1 teaspoon vanilla, divided
1 (9-inch) unbaked graham cracker crust
1 cup sour cream

Combine cream cheese and 1 cup sugar; beat until smooth. Add eggs, 1 at a time, beating well after each addition. Add ½ teaspoon vanilla. Pour into graham cracker crust. Bake 30 minutes at 350°. Cool 10 minutes. Combine sour cream, ¼ cup sugar and ½ teaspoon vanilla. Pour sour cream topping over pie. Bake an additional 15 minutes. Cool.

PEACH TOPPING:

5 to 6 large, fresh peaches
2½ tablespoons cornstarch

½ cup sugar

Cook all ingredients in saucepan over medium heat until thickened. Spread on pie evenly. Chill thoroughly before serving.

Courtney Blackburn
Peach Festival

Peach Festival Hay Toss

Clara's Cream Pie

The cafe was founded in 1958 and is located south of Waynoka on US 281.

PIE CRUST:

1¼ cups all-purpose flour
¼ teaspoon salt
1½ tablespoons sugar

½ cup butter-flavored Crisco
⅛ to ¼ cup ice water

Combine flour, salt and sugar. Cut in Crisco, your hands or a pastry cutter, until mixture is crumbly, like very coarse cornmeal. Add ice water, a little at a time, until mixture comes together forming a dough. Bring dough together into a ball. Flatten it slightly to form a round shape. Wrap in plastic and chill in the refrigerator about 30 minutes. Roll into a 10- to 11-inch circle to make a 9-inch pie.

CREAM PIE FILLING:

3 cups milk
4 eggs, separated (reserve whites for meringue)
1 cup sugar

Heaping ¼ cup cornstarch
1 teaspoon vanilla
Tiny pinch salt

Put milk on slow heat. Separate eggs. Beat yolks and sugar to creamy. Add a small amount of milk to yolks and sugar mixture. Add cornstarch. Add to milk and bring to boil, stirring. Remove from heat; add vanilla and salt. Pour into baked pie crust.

MERINGUE:

Beat egg whites with ¼ cup sugar until stiff peaks form. Spread on cream filling and bake 8 to 10 minutes at 400°.

FILLING VARIATIONS:

Coconut Cream: add 1 cup coconut

Cherry Cream : Top cream pie with cherry pie filling

Peanut Butter: Add peanut butter to cream mixture

Chocolate: Add ¼ cup cocoa mixed with ¼ cup sugar.

Clara Miller, Miller's Cafe, Waynoka
Cimarron River Stampede Rodeo

Cimarron River Stampede Rodeo

August

Waynoka Rodeo Arena • Waynoka
580-824-0029
www.cimarronriverstampede.com • www.waynokachamber.com

Waynoka sits next to the Little Sahara State Park, which is one of the nation's best sand dune parks, often referred to as "America's Sandbox". Waynoka welcomes more than 250,000 visitors annually. Some come to experience fun in the sand, some to visit the "Den of Death" at the annual Rattlesnake Hunt, others are hunters looking for that trophy whitetail deer, and many come to visit our beautifully restored Harvey House, which includes an Air Rail Museum.

Every year, the second weekend in August, is a time of great excitement and fun in Waynoka. Hundreds, sometimes thousands, gather for the Cimarron River Stampede Rodeo. In the early years, this rodeo was held in a pasture and featured local area cowhands with roping skills. In 1946, the rodeo got its name and became one of the first organized rodeos in the area. Waynoka's rodeo has come a long way! In 2011, the 75th Annual Cimarron River Stampede Rodeo boasted the finest stock available, some of the rankest bulls ever seen, cowboys from far and wide, and some very entertaining banter between the rodeo clown and the announcer. The whole weekend is a big celebration in Waynoka, with events downtown to boot. Come experience rodeo at it's finest at the oldest rodeo in the area!

"Honoring our past while celebrating our future'"

Route 66
Pecan Pie

1 unbaked pie crust
1 cup light corn syrup
1 cup light brown sugar, lightly
   packed
½ teaspoon salt
5 tablespoons unsalted butter,
   melted
1 teaspoon vanilla extract
3 large eggs, lightly beaten
2 cups pecan halves, toasted
Whipped cream, for topping

Preheat oven to 375°. Place pie crust in a 9-inch pie plate and bake 9 to 10 minutes. Allow crust to cool completely. Whisk together corn syrup, brown sugar, salt, butter and vanilla in a medium bowl. Add eggs and continue to whisk. Take ½ cup pecan halves, chop fine and spread evenly on pie crust. Chop remaining pecans in larger pieces, adding ½ cup to corn syrup mixture. Pour filling into pie crust, and top with remaining pecans. Bake 40 to 50 minutes. Allow to cool completely before serving. Top with whipped cream.

Route 66 Pecan & Fun Fest

Route 66 Pecan & Fun Fest

October

The Nut House
Claremore
918-266-1604
www.route66nuthouse.com

Pecan pie eating contest, beautiful and unique crafts, and a car show are the highlights of the Route 66 Pecan & Fun Fest. Right off of Route 66, The Nut House sets the stage for a wonderful fall event for the whole family. There are inflatable jumps for the kids, and they can pick out and decorate their very own pumpkin. Parents can troll through booths filled with handcrafted wares just in time for the holiday gift-giving season. After the festivities wind down it's time to sit and enjoy a down-home barbecue dinner. After the sun sets, the Sock Hop gets underway, complete with pop hits and oldies performed live by local entertainers.

The Nut House

Located in Claremore on old Highway 66 is a log cabin made from pecan wood. Aptly named The Nut House, it was established 40 years ago selling pecans and has grown into a one-stop shop for deli-style meals, candy and fudge, gift baskets and, of course, nuts. They are open year round, stop by and say hello.

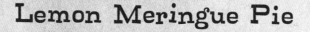

Lemon Meringue Pie

FILLING:

1½ cups sugar

¼ cup plus 2 tablespoons
  cornstarch

1 tablespoon flour

⅛ teaspoon salt

½ cup lemon juice

1 tablespoon grated lemon rind

1 cup cold water

3 egg yolks, well beaten (use
  whites for meringue)

1½ cups boiling water

1 (9-inch) pie shell, baked

Blend sugar, cornstarch, flour and salt in medium saucepan. Add lemon juice, rind, cold water, beaten egg yolks, blending until very smooth. Add boiling water. Bring to a boil over medium heat, stirring constantly, then boil 2 to 3 minutes. Remove from heat. Stir filling occasionally until warm. When cool, add to baked pie shell.

MERINGUE:

4 egg whites

½ teaspoon cream of tartar

⅔ cups sugar

Beat egg whites and cream of tartar until soft peaks form. Add sugar gradually, beating until stiff. Apply to top pie filling making sure to flip a few curls for panache. Bake at 350° for 10 to 13 minutes.

Susen Foster, Planet Earth Jewelry

Double Layer Peach Cobbler

FILLING:

8 cups peeled and sliced fresh
  peaches
2 to 4 tablespoons all-purpose
  flour

2 cups sugar
½ teaspoon ground nutmeg
  (optional)
⅓ cup melted butter

Preheat oven to 400°. Combine peaches, flour, sugar and nutmeg in a large pan. Bring to a boil and cook over low heat 10 minutes or until tender. Remove from heat and add butter.

PASTRY:

2⅔ cups flour
2 teaspoons salt

1 cup shortening
6 tablespoons ice water

Mix flour and salt, cut in shortening; add ice water and toss with fork until well blended. Turn out on floured board and knead 3 or 4 times. Roll out ½ pastry to ⅛-inch thickness. Cut pastry into a 9x13-inch rectangle. Spoon ½ peaches into a 9x13-inch buttered baking dish and top with pastry. Bake 23 minutes, until golden brown. Remove from oven and spoon remaining peaches over baked pastry. Roll out remaining pastry and cut into ½-inch strips. Arrange in lattice design over peaches. Brush strips with melted butter. Sprinkle with sugar. Return to oven 10 to 15 minutes.

Anita Henry Warden
Peach Festival

Peach Amaretto Cobbler

FLAKY VODKA CRUST:

3 cups flour
1 teaspoon salt
2 tablespoons sugar
1½ sticks unsalted butter, chilled

½ cup chilled shortening
¼ cup cold water
¼ cup cold 80 proof vodka

Combine dry ingredients in a bowl and mix together. In a separate bowl, put 1½ cups mixture with butter and shortening and blend with pastry into dry ingredients until mixture resembles coarse breadcrumbs. Add remaining 1 cup dry mixture and blend with pastry cutter. In another bowl, mix vodka and water together. Sprinkle liquids over mixture and combine with a fork until dough holds together. Place dough in plastic wrap and chill at least 30 minutes. Using well-floured parchment paper roll dough out between sheets starting in the middle with short strokes. Prepare a 12-inch Dutch oven by covering bottom with parchment strips. Press ⅔ pastry crust (reserve rest for top) into bottom and halfway up side.

COBBLER FILLING:

2 cans peach pie filling
¼ cup flour
2 cups sugar
½ teaspoon vanilla

¼ cup amaretto
Cinnamon and sugar
Butter
1 egg white

Combine peaches, flour, sugar and vanilla. Add amaretto and gently mix. Pour filling into pastry crust and sprinkle with cinnamon sugar. Place butter pats on top. Roll out top crust and place over filling. Trim crust as desired. Lightly beat egg white and brush on top of crust. Sprinkle with sugar. Bake 55 to 60 minutes with 10 coals on bottom and 20 coals on top, rotating oven and lid every 15 minutes to avoid hot spots. When cobbler is golden brown, remove from coals.

Curtis & Gaye Ann Grace
Charlie Adams Day

Marshmallow Apple Crisp

4 cups sliced apples
¾ cup flour
½ cup sugar
1 teaspoon cinnamon

¼ teaspoon salt
¼ cup water
½ cup margarine
1½ cups mini marshmallows

Preheat oven to 350°. Place apples in a 10x6-inch baking dish. In separate bowl, combine flour, sugar, cinnamon, salt and water. Cut in margarine until it resembles coarse crumbs. Sprinkle on apples. Bake 35 to 40 minutes or until apples are tender. Sprinkle apples with mini marshmallows and place under broiler until melted and light brown.

Jane Apple
Hitching Post Bed & Breakfast

Chocolatey Raspberry Crumb Bars

1 cup butter or margarine, softened
2 cups all-purpose flour
½ cup lightly packed brown sugar
¼ teaspoon salt
1 (12-ounce) package semi-sweet
  chocolate morsels, divided

1 (14-ounce) can sweetened
  condensed milk
½ cup chopped nuts (optional)
½ cup seedless raspberry jam

Preheat oven to 350°. Grease 9x13-inch pan. Beat butter in large mixing bowl until creamy. Add flour, sugar and salt until crumbly. With floured fingers, press 1¾ cups crumb mixture onto bottom of prepared baking pan, reserve the remaining mixture. Bake 10 to 12 minutes or until edges are golden brown. Microwave 1 cup morsels and sweetened condensed milk in medium microwave-safe bowl on high for 1 minute; stir. Microwave at additional 10 to 20 second intervals, stirring until smooth. Spread over hot crust. Stir nuts into remaining flour mixture; sprinkle over chocolate layer. Drop spoonfuls of raspberry jam over flour mixture. Sprinkle with remaining morsels. Bake 25 to 30 minutes or until center is set. Cool completely. Cut into bars. Yields about 3 dozen bars.

Sondra Martin
Bedstead Retreat

Nancy's Best Shortbread

Submitted by long time volunteer, Nancy Blass, this is a favorite treat served at many volunteer meetings!

1 pound butter, softened
2 cups sugar
4¼ cups flour

Cream together butter and sugar. Work flour into butter and sugar mixture using hands. (Warm hands done on a warm, humid day makes for better shortbread.) Work it until all flour is absorbed and dough is formed into a solid ball. Cut into quarters and pat into rounds approximately 8 inches in diameter and rather thick (1 inch thick). This works best using a wood mold. Mine has a Scottish thistle and looks quite pretty when done. If using a mold, oil the surface, removing any excess, then coat with sugar before pressing dough into mold. Carefully drop formed dough onto ungreased cookie sheet, pretty side up. Trim outside edges to neaten into uniform shape. Bake at 325° until outer edges barely turn golden, about 25 minutes. Cut into squares while still warm. Cool before removing from cookie sheet as it will harden as it cools.

This shortbread is not overly crumbly and eats more like a cookie. From California to Oklahoma, this recipe has received rave reviews.

Nancy Blass
Medieval Fair

Medieval Fair of Norman

First Weekend in April

Reaves Park • Norman
800-767-7260 • www.medievalfair.org
Find The Medieval Fair of Norman on Facebook

Held annually since 1977, The Medieval Fair is a modern reproduction of fairs held in Europe during the Middle Ages. Experience the magic of days gone by with fine art, food fit for a king, games and entertainment for all ages. Merriment abounds with jousting, storytellers, jugglers, musicians, dancing and human chess games. Learn something new at every turn in the road at the educational exhibits and craft demonstrations. The Medieval Fair comes to life for three days at Reaves Park (2501 South Jenkins Ave.) in Norman, Oklahoma the first weekend of April. More than 200 fine artisans from 30 different states and over 100 performers on 7 stages help to recreate a medieval market fair. Admission is free and nearby parking is available for $5 at the Lloyd Noble Center. It is made possible in part by the Norman Arts Council Grant, the City of Norman and the University of Oklahoma.

Snickerdoodle Cookies

½ cup butter, softened
1 cup plus 4 tablespoons sugar
¼ teaspoon baking soda
1 egg
½ teaspoon vanilla
1½ cups all-purpose flour
1½ teaspoons cinnamon

Preheat oven to 375°. Mix together butter, 1 cup sugar and baking soda. Beat in egg and vanilla; blend well. Slowly blend in flour, allow it to sit 45 minutes in a refrigerator. In separate bowl, mix 4 tablespoons of sugar and cinnamon. Make balls of dough and roll in sugar cinnamon mixture; place on cookie sheet. Bake 10 minutes or until golden brown.

Catina Jordan
Heartland Flyer – Amtrak

Heartland Flyer Amtrak

100 South E. K. Gaylord Boulevard • Oklahoma City
800-USA-RAIL • www.heartlandflyer.com

All Aboard! The Heartland Flyer is Oklahoma's passenger train, making one round trip daily between Oklahoma City and Fort Worth. Stops along the way are Norman, Purcell, Pauls Valley, Ardmore, and Gainesville.

There had been decades without a passenger train in the state, and that changed in 1999. Amtrak and the Oklahoma Department of Transportation joined forces to reignite the rail service, and in June the 11 car Flyer took its inaugural run out of Fort Worth. After only one month of service, the new train had transported over 11,000 passengers.

Superliner Coaches and a Superliner II Coach/Cafe Car make up the Heartland Flyer. Each of the coaches feature an upper level coach section with spacious reclining seats, complete with individual reading lights and large windows. The lower level of the two Superliner Coaches features 12 wheel-chair accessible seats on one end and restrooms on the other end. On the lower level of the Superliner II Coach is a full-service cafe car with an attendant and featuring snacks, sandwiches, soft drinks, cocktails, souvenirs and sofa style seating where guests can visit and watch the scenery glide by.

Call or visit the website for schedules, tickets and to learn about the many events held throughout the year.

Granny Brenda's
Chocolate Chip Patties

¾ cup light brown sugar
¾ cup sugar
1 cup shortening
2 large eggs
1 teaspoon vanilla
2¼ cups flour
1 teaspoon salt
1 teaspoon baking soda
1 teaspoon cinnamon
1 cup pecan pieces
1¼ cup semi-sweet chocolate chips

Preheat oven to 375°. Combine both sugars in a mixing bowl; cream in shortening. Add eggs and vanilla; mix. Add flour, salt, baking soda and cinnamon; mix well. Dough should be very stiff. Stir in pecans and chocolate chips. Drop by heaping spoonful's onto ungreased baking sheet. Bake 8 minutes. (Do not over bake.) Makes 3 dozen cookies.

McAlester Wild West Festival

Mistletoe Troop Sugar Cookies

The Girl Scouts Mistletoe Troop of Muskogee was the first in the world to sell cookies as a fundraiser. Within a few years of their first sale in 1917, Girl Scouts cookies were a national fundraising effort and are now a world-wide enterprise.

2¾ cups all-purpose flour
1 teaspoon baking soda
½ teaspoon baking powder
1¼ cups butter, softened

1½ cups sugar
1 egg
1 teaspoon vanilla extract

Preheat oven to 375°. In a small bowl, mix flour, baking soda and baking powder. Set aside. In a large bowl, cream butter and sugar until smooth. Beat in egg and vanilla. Gradually blend in the dry ingredients. Roll rounded teaspoonfuls of dough into balls, and place onto ungreased cookie sheets. Bake 8 to 10 minutes, or until golden. Let rest on cookie sheet briefly before removing to cool on wire racks.

Heritage Days: A Living History Museum

Mrs. Frost's Cookies

4 cups flour
½ teaspoon baking soda
1 cup lard
2 cups sugar

2 eggs
1 cup buttermilk
Nutmeg to taste

In a large bowl, combine flour and baking soda. Set aside. Mix lard and sugar until smooth. Add eggs and buttermilk and beat until fluffy, about 2 minutes. Gradually add flour mixture until dough is stiff. (May use more flour, if necessary.) Form dough into a disk. Refrigerate, wrapped, for at least 1 hour and up to 3 days. When ready to bake, preheat oven to 350°. On a floured surface, roll out disk ½-inch thick. Cut into shapes and place on parchment-lined baking sheets; refrigerate until firm. Sprinkle with nutmeg and bake until just beginning to brown, 12 to 15 minutes.

Mrs. Overholser, circa 1903
Overholser Mansion

My Favorite Oatmeal-Raisin Cookies

1½ cups packed dark brown sugar
½ cup butter, softened
½ cup canola oil
1½ teaspoons vanilla
1 egg, beaten
1 teaspoon cinnamon
2 cups quick cooking oats
1½ cups all-purpose flour
1 teaspoon baking soda
¼ teaspoon salt
1 cup raisins (or chocolate chips)
1 cup chopped nuts

Preheat oven to 350°. In a large bowl, stir brown sugar, butter and oil until well blended. Stir in vanilla and egg and continue beating until light. Stir in cinnamon, oats, flour, baking soda and salt; mix well. Add raisins and nuts and blend into mixture. Drop dough by mounded teaspoons onto ungreased cookie sheet and press lightly to flatten. Bake 9 to 11 minutes or until golden brown. Remove from cookie sheet to wire rack. Yield: 4 dozen medium-sized cookies.

Marian Clark
Arcadia Round Barn

Arcadia Round Barn

Located about 6 miles east of I-35 (Edmond),
on old Route 66 • Arcadia
405-396-0824 • www.arcadiaroundbarn.com

Museum and Gift Shop open daily 10 am to 5 pm
Free admission

Arcadia Round Barn in Arcadia, Oklahoma is the most photographed landmark on Route 66. Designed and built in 1898 by Oklahoma pioneer William H. Odor, it became a community gathering place along with being a regular barn sheltering cattle, oxen and mules and storing hay. After suffering through decades of neglect and some modifications that compromised its structural integrity, the barn's roof collapsed in 1988. Luther Robison and a group of retirees named "The Over the Hill Gang" restored the barn back to its former glory. It now houses a museum and gift shop along with hosting community events throughout the year.

Kolache

2 packages dry yeast
⅔ cup butter-flavored Crisco
¾ cup sugar
2 teaspoons salt

1 egg plus 3 egg yolks
1 teaspoon lemon juice
1¾ cups scalded milk
6 cups flour, divided

Mix yeast with ¼ cup lukewarm water, set aside. With mixer, cream together Crisco, sugar and salt. Add 1 egg plus 3 egg yolks, 1 at a time and continue mixing. Add lemon juice, milk and 4 cups flour. Mix well. Add yeast and rest of flour. Dough should not feel stiff. Place dough in a greased bowl and let rise until double. Punch dough down and let set 10 minutes.

Roll dough into smooth balls the size of a large walnut. Place balls about 2 inches apart on greased cookie sheets. Let rise until each ball doubles in size. Make an indention in center of each ball by stretching with fingertips. The indention is to hold the fruit filling. The kolache will look similar to a pie shell. Fill each Kolache with fruit filling (see below), let rise for about 30 minutes. Cover each Kolache with posipka (see next page) and bake in 375° oven about 20 minutes. When you take pan out of oven, brush sides of dough with melted butter. Makes about 4 dozen.

Any type of fresh or dried fruit filling can be used for kolaches. Blend and cook fruit as for a cobbler, or use fruit pie filling such as cherry. The authentic fillings include cherry, apricot, prune, poppy seed, pear and apple.

POSIPKA, TOPPING FOR KOLACHES

½ cup sugar
½ cup flour

⅓ cup melted butter

Mix together with hands until crumbly. Sprinkle on top of Kolache filling before baking. You can also add finely chopped pecans.

Lillie Bartos
Kolache Festival

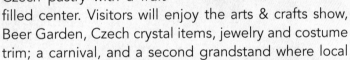

Kolache Festival

First Saturday in May

Prague
405-567-4866
www.praguekolachefestival.com

Polka music, festive Czech costumes and the aroma of foods greet visitors to the annual Kolache Festival, a free event named for the Czech pastry with a fruit-filled center. Visitors will enjoy the arts & crafts show, Beer Garden, Czech crystal items, jewelry and costume trim; a carnival, and a second grandstand where local entertainers perform. A Czech Costume Contest is held during the festival for all age groups. The Kolache Festival royalty crowning features the new queen, junior queen, princess and prince. These events are a great opportunity

to view the beautiful and exquisite embroidery and bead work featured in the costumes, each one unique in its own design. There is also a homemade wine, beer, kolache and bread contest open to the public. Don't miss the Prague Czech Folk Dancers or the fun parade and be sure to stay for the polka street dance and the spectacular fireworks display at the end of the night.

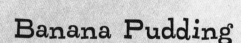

Banana Pudding

1 box vanilla wafers
1 cup sugar
½ cup all-purpose flour
½ teaspoon salt
4 egg yolks

2 cups milk
1 teaspoon vanilla extract
1 tablespoon butter (not
   margarine)
4 to 5 ripe bananas, sliced

Preheat oven to 375°. Line bottom of a 9x9-inch baking dish with vanilla wafers. Combine sugar, flour and salt in a bowl and mix well. In a large saucepan, beat egg yolks well. Over medium heat, add flour mixture, milk and vanilla to egg yolks, stirring constantly. Bring to a boil. When mixture begins to thicken, add butter and continue to stir. Continue to cook and stir until mixture is consistency of pudding. Remove from heat. Place a layer of banana slices (using about ½) in baking dish on top of vanilla wafers. Pour ½ pudding over bananas, spreading evenly. Repeat layers, beginning with wafers.

MERINGUE:

4 egg whites, room temperature
¼ teaspoon cream of tartar

5 tablespoons sugar
½ teaspoon vanilla extract

Beat egg whites at high speed until they form soft peaks. Add cream of tartar and continue beating. Gradually add sugar and beat until stiff peaks form. Fold in vanilla and spread meringue over banana pudding layers. Bake 12 to 15 minutes, until meringue has golden brown tips.

The Meers Store and Restaurant

The Meers Store and Restaurant

Meers

580-429-8051 • www.meersstore.com

Hours of Operation:
Sun – Thurs 10:30 am to 8:30 pm,
Fri & Sat 10:30 am to 9 pm
Closed on Tuesdays

A trip through the state is not complete without a stop at this world-renowned restaurant. The Meers Store and Restaurant is home to the "Best Burger in Oklahoma".

The Meers Store and Restaurant serves a delicious selection of steaks, barbecue, home-baked bread, and desserts including homemade ice cream. Don't have time to sit and eat? Longhorn beef steaks, hamburger meat, barbecued brisket, spare ribs, polish sausage, chicken and thick-sliced bacon are available in the store.

During the gold rush, Meers was a bustling town of miners seeking gold in the Wichita Mountains. All that remains today is this famous restaurant, a family of six people, eight cats and a dog.

Directions: Located on Highway 115, 1½ miles north of the Wichita Mountain Wildlife Refuge. Take I-44 to Hwy 49, travel west about 4 miles, to Hwy 58. Turn to the North for about 5 miles to the turn-off to Meers (follow the signs). Now turn to the West for 4 miles and you're there.

Bailey's Croissants

1 (8-ounce) package cream cheese, softened
½ cup powdered sugar
½ cup Bailey's Irish Cream
2 packages crescent rolls

Combine cream cheese, sugar and Bailey's. Beat until light and fluffy. Unroll and separate crescents. Spread mixture evenly over each crescent. Roll up and cook according to package directions.

GLAZE:

1 cup powdered sugar
¼ cup Bailey's

Mix together and drizzle over warm crescents.

Virginia Scott
Holiday in the Park

Oklahoma Po' Boy Pudding

2 eggs plus 1 egg yolk
¾ cup sugar
3 tablespoons flour
2 tablespoons baking powder
¼ tablespoon salt
¼ cup chopped walnuts or
   chopped pecans

2 red apples, seeded, peeled,
   cored and chopped
1 tablespoon vanilla extract
1 cup heavy cream, whipped to
   a peak

Butter a 9-inch pie pan and preheat oven to 350°. In large bowl, beat eggs and sugar until creamy. Blend in flour, baking powder and salt. Fold in nuts, apples and vanilla. Pour into pie pan and bake 30 minutes. Remove from oven and let cool 15 minutes. Serve with whipped cream.

J.M. Davis Arms & Historical Museum

Southern Baklava

4 cups chopped pecans
½ cup sugar
1 teaspoon ground cinnamon

1 (16-ounce) package frozen
    phyllo dough, thawed
2 cups butter, melted

In food processor, blend together pecans, sugar and cinnamon to make filling. Brush bottom of a 15x10x1-inch baking pan with some of the melted butter. Unfold phyllo dough. Keep phyllo covered, removing sheets as you need them. Layer 10 phyllo sheets in pan 2 at a time, generously brushing each pair with melted butter as you layer, and allowing phyllo to extend up sides of pan. Sprinkle about 1½ cups filling on top of phyllo. Repeat layering phyllo sheets and filling twice. Layer remaining phyllo sheets atop third layer of filling, continuing to brush each sheet with butter before adding the next phyllo sheet. Drizzle remaining butter over top layers. Trim edges of phyllo to fit pan. Set in fridge for 30 minutes to set butter to make easier to cut. Using a sharp knife, cut through all layers to make 60 diamond, triangle or square-shaped pieces. An easy tip is to cut squares then cut diagonally across the squares, creating triangles. Bake in a 325° oven for 45 to 50 minutes or until golden. Slightly cool in pan on a wire rack.

SYRUP:

1½ cups brown sugar
1 cup water

¼ cup orange juice
1 teaspoon ground cinnamon

While baklava is baking, make syrup. In a medium saucepan stir together brown sugar, water, orange juice and cinnamon. Bring mixture a boil. Reduce heat. Simmer, uncovered, for 20 minutes. Pour syrup over warm baklava in pan. Cool completely. Place in an airtight container and store at room temperature up to 3 days or freeze up to 1 month. Thaw at room temperature for 30 minutes before serving. Makes about 60 baklava.

Aaron's Gate Country Getaways

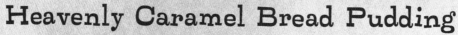

Heavenly Caramel Bread Pudding

1 loaf white bread
6 cups heavy cream
7 eggs
½ cup cinnamon

½ cup vanilla extract
3 cups sugar
2 bananas, sliced
Caramel Topping

Cut bread into cubes and spread evenly in a 9x13-inch baking pan. In a separate bowl, mix heavy cream, eggs, cinnamon, vanilla extract and sugar by hand. When the mixture tastes like vanilla ice cream, pour over bread cubes and press into bread. Be sure to press mixture into bread rather than stirring it with the bread. Evenly distribute sliced bananas on top of pressed mixture. Bake at 350° for 30 minutes. Serve warm with caramel topping to taste.

Chef Chad Striplin
Sheraton Midwest City Hotel at the Reed Conference Center
Midwest City Convention and Visitors Bureau

Midwest City's Holiday Lights Spectacular

The Friday before Thanksgiving through December 30th
Sun – Thurs 6 pm to 10 pm • Fri & Sat 6 pm to 11 pm

Joe B. Barnes Regional Park
8700 East Reno, Midwest City
405-739-1293 • www.midwestcityok.org

Midwest City knows how to celebrate Christmas at Holiday Lights Spectacular! The sparkle of the season turns stunning as over 1.5 million lights and 90 brilliant displays create an enchanted winter wonderland right in the heart of Joe B. Barnes Regional Park. The one-of-a-kind Santa fly-fishing in a 15-foot waterfall and majestic 118-foot LED Christmas tree topped with an 8-foot lighted star are sights to see. The tunnel of lights that stretches 17-feet tall and 22-feet wide is sure to delight. The holiday spirit is captivating during the 1.5 mile long drive that creates Oklahoma's largest animated drive-through lights display. The newest display, "Illumination Celebration," is a dancing forest of extravagant lights choreographed to favorite Christmas melodies.

There are romantic and family oriented carriage rides available on Friday and Saturday nights.

With easy access from I-40 and just 10 minutes east of Oklahoma City, families will want to make this an annual tradition for years to come. And remember admission is always free!

Root Beer Bread Pudding

5 eggs
2½ tablespoons vanilla extract
¾ cups root beer syrup
6½ cups heavy cream

1¼ cups sugar
2¼ cups raisins
2½ loaves Texas toast, cubed
1½ cups brown sugar

Spray a large casserole dish with pan spray. Mix eggs, vanilla, root beer syrup, cream, sugar and raisins in a large bowl. Add cubed Texas toast and mix just until incorporated. Pour into casserole dish. Top with brown sugar and bake at 350° for 35 minutes. Yields 12 servings.

GLAZE FOR BREAD PUDDING:

3 ounces butter
¾ cups brown sugar

4½ cups heavy cream
½ cup root beer syrup

Melt butter and brown sugar together in a saucepan. Whisk until smooth and simmering. Add cream and root beer syrup and allow to reduce by ⅓, about 15 minutes. Yields 3 quarts.

Pops

Pops

660 West Highway 66 • Arcadia
405-928-POPS or 877-266-POPS • www.pops66.com

Pops is Food, Fuel and Fizz all wrapped into one fantastic architectural structure, showcasing a 66 foot tall pop bottle—a Route 66 icon. Each night LED lights transform it into a dazzling light show with an array of colors and patterns that salute the world's greatest variety of soda pop inside with over 600 selections from all over the world. A fun, bright, family-friendly atmosphere, Pops is open 7 days a week for lunch and dinner with great burgers featuring 100% Black Angus beef, sandwiches, salads, chicken fried steak, hand dipped shakes, malts, endless float combinations and more. Breakfast is served Saturday and Sunday mornings only.

Just a short drive down Historic Route 66, Pops is a unique destination stop northeast of Oklahoma City.

Almond Truffle Brownies

1 package fudge brownie mix
½ cup water
1 egg
½ cup vegetable oil
¾ cup chopped almonds

Combine ingredients in a large bowl. Pour into a greased 9x13-inch baking pan. Bake at 350° for 23 to 25 minutes or until a toothpick inserted near the center comes out clean (do not over-bake). Cool on a wire rack.

FILLING:

1 cup semi-sweet chocolate chips
1 (8-ounce) package cream cheese, softened
⅓ cup powdered sugar
2 tablespoons milk
½ teaspoon almond extract

In a microwave, melt chocolate chips; stir until smooth. In a large mixing bowl, beat cream cheese and powdered sugar. Add milk, almond extract and melted chips; mix well. Spread over brownies. Refrigerate 1 hour until firm.

TOPPING:

½ cup semi-sweet chocolate chips
¼ cup heavy whipping cream
½ cup sliced almonds

In a small saucepan, melt chips and cream over low heat, stirring occasionally. Spread over filling. Sprinkle with almonds. Refrigerate at least 1 hour longer before cutting.

Sandra Maddux, Cooking with Cheese
Watonga Cheese Festival

City of Watonga

Watonga Chamber of Commerce
505 South Clarence Nash Boulevard
580-623-5452 • www.watongachamber.com

For hiking, fishing and camping in the great outdoors or strolling through quaint gift and antique stores, Watonga is the perfect location for a weekend getaway. Home of Roman Nose State Park, the outdoor enthusiast can enjoy year round springs and unique canyon views within the park and from the challenging 18-hole Roman Nose Golf Course. For the shoppers, Main Street has several antique stores, gift boutiques and a cozy coffee shop for a mid-afternoon break. And not to leave out the history buffs, the T.B. Ferguson Home, built in 1907 by the 6th territorial governor, is open for tours, offering wonderful displays of antiques in this richly restored gem. Be sure to take in the 1901 Presbyterian Chapel and the 1906, copper domed courthouse.

Cowboy Mint Candy

1 (8-ounce) package cream cheese, softened
1 (32-ounce) bag powdered sugar
A few drops mint extract
A few drops red food coloring

Mix cream cheese and powdered sugar. Add mint extract and food coloring; mix well. Spread onto flat, greased cookie sheet and let cool. Break into pieces and eat.

Jane Apple
Hitching Post Bed & Breakfast

Microwave Peanut Patties

2 cups sugar
½ cup water
Dash salt
½ cup light corn syrup

1½ to 2 cups peanuts
2 tablespoons butter
1 teaspoon vanilla
Red food coloring

In a microwave-safe bowl, combine sugar, water, salt and corn syrup. Place in microwave and cook 3 to 5 minutes. Add peanuts and stir. Place back into microwave and cook 10 minutes or until mixture reaches 234° (may use candy thermometer after removing from microwave). Add butter, vanilla and 2 to 3 drops of food coloring. Stir until creamy and begins to thicken. Drop by spoonful on greased cookie sheet.

Jane Apple
Hitching Post Bed & Breakfast

Easy Peanut Brittle

1 cup sugar
1 cup light corn syrup

2 cups raw peanuts
1 teaspoon baking soda

Combine sugar, corn syrup and peanuts. Cook over medium heat until golden brown. Peanuts will smell done and pop. Add baking soda and quickly pour onto greased cookie sheet.

Jan Watson
Holiday in the Park

Toffee Treat

Saltine crackers
1 cup chopped nuts
1 cup real butter
1 cup brown sugar
1 (12-ounce) package semi-sweet chocolate chips

Line an 11x17-inch flat pan with heavy foil. Cover with saltine crackers. Sprinkle with chopped nuts. In a saucepan, melt butter. Add brown sugar and bring to a boil. Boil exactly 3 minutes. Pour over crackers and spread. Bake 5 minutes at 350°. Sprinkle with chocolate chips and return to oven for 10 seconds. Spread and refrigerate. Break into pieces to serve.

Lila C. Singleton
American Banjo Museum

Cheese Fudge

1 pound margarine
1 pound processed
   cheese (Velveeta works
   best)
1 teaspoon vanilla
1 cup cocoa
4 pounds powdered
   sugar (½ pound more
   for firmer fudge)
2 cups chopped pecans
   or walnuts, optional

Melt margarine and cheese in double boiler. Add vanilla, cocoa and powdered sugar into melted cheese mixture. Stir in pecans. Mix well. Press in buttered 9x13-inch pan and cool.

Watonga Cheese Festival

Watonga Cheese Festival

Second Weekend in October

Downtown on Main Street
Watonga
580-623-3367
www.watongacheesefestival.com

The Watonga Cheese Festival is held the second weekend in October on Main Street. Its namesake is true to form, with a cheese tasting line, a cheese food contest, and a rat race. Two large tents are home to vendors of all types, including "Made in Oklahoma" vendors and an armory of craft vendors. There is professional entertainment, an art and fiber show, a parade, "Race the Rail" bicycle race, a classic car show, food concessions, children's art, family amusements, demonstrations and much, much more.

Brownies

10 ounces bittersweet chocolate
4 ounces butter
6 eggs
2 cups sugar
2 teaspoons vanilla extract
½ cup flour
¼ cup cocoa powder
2 teaspoons baking powder
1 teaspoon salt
½ cup sour cream
6 ounces bittersweet chocolate, cut in ¼ inch chunks
  (may use chips)
1 cup chopped walnuts

Preheat oven to 300°. Melt 10 ounces bittersweet chocolate and butter together over a water bath. Combine eggs, sugar and vanilla and whisk until light yellow. Whip warm chocolate into eggs and sugar. Sift together flour, cocoa, baking powder and salt. Add to wet mixture. Fold together until smooth. Add sour cream and whip until smooth. Pour into buttered 9x13-inch pan. Spread evenly. Sprinkle with chocolate chunks and nuts. Bake until firm but still moist in center, about 50 minutes. Cool before cutting.

Chef Neil Lindenbaum
Paul's Place Steakhouse

Indexes

A traditional symbol of the winter holidays is also Oklahoma's official floral emblem. Mistletoe was adopted by the state in 1893.

Index of Events & Destinations

C

Chuck Wagon Gathering & Children's Cowboy Festival

Enid Lights Up the Plains

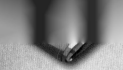

Overholser Mansion

Turnip Festival

*Rope spinning at
Will Rogers & Wiley Post Fly-In*

Index of Recipes

Turnips!

After we had made the race
We hadn't much to feed our face.
The old cow's milk had turned to whey;
Our few old hens refused to lay.
Our flour and bacon both ran out;
The beans we planted failed to sprout;
We had no bread and grease to sop,
But our turnips made a bumper crop.

To purchase grub we had no kale;
For turnips there was sure no sale.
Just one thing left and that we chose,
Eat turnips-or turn up our toes.
We had cooked and turnips raw
Turnip stew and turnip slaw,
Turnips boiled and turnips fried,
Turnips canned and turnips dried.

Turnips flat and turnips round,
Turnips spoiled and turnips sound;
Turnips white and turnips red,
Turnips piled and turnips spread.
Turnips large and turnips small,
Turnips winter, spring, and fall.
Turnips hot and turnips cold;
Turnips new and turnips old.

Turnips fresh and turnips stale,
Turnips by the ton and bale,
Turnips baked and turnips boiled,
Turnips clean and turnips soiled;
Turnips thrown at neighbors dogs,
Turnips fed to cows and hogs.
Turnip soup and turnip greens,
Turnips without meat or beans;

We thanked our stars that turnips grew,
For turnips surely pulled us through.
Turnips soft and turnips hard,
Turnips minus salt or lard;
Turnips smooth and turnips rough,
Turnips tender, turnips tough.

Turnips sliced and turnips scraped,
Turnips every size and shape;
Turnips sweet and turnips strong,
Turnips short and turnips long.
Turnips good and turnips bad,
The sight of turnips made us mad.
For something else we daily wished,
But nothing else to us was dished.

Though pocketbooks and cows were dry,
Yet somehow, someway we got by.
On turnips, sure, we nearly choked.
Without those turnips, we'd have
croaked.

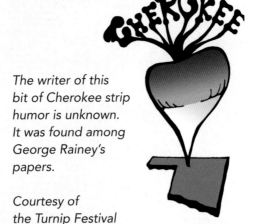

*The writer of this
bit of Cherokee strip
humor is unknown.
It was found among
George Rainey's
papers.*

*Courtesy of
the Turnip Festival*

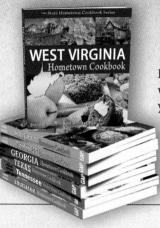

Eat & Explore Cookbook Series

Discover community celebrations and unique destinations, as they share their favorite recipes.

This series is a favorite of local cooks, armchair travelers, and cookbook collectors across the nation.

Arkansas   **Minnesota**   **Ohio**   **Oklahoma**

Explore the distinct flavor of each state by savoring 200 favorite local recipes. In addition, fun festivals, exciting events, unique attractions, and fascinating tourist destinations are profiled throughout the book with everything you need to plan your family's next getaway.

EACH: $18.95 • 240 to 272 pages
7x9 • paperbound

North Carolina   **Virginia**   **Washington**

ORDER FORM

Mail to: Great American Publishers • 171 Lone Pine Church Road • Lena, MS 39094
Or call us toll-free 1.888.854.5954 to order by check or credit card

❑ Check Enclosed
Charge to: ❑ Visa ❑ MC ❑ AmEx ❑ Disc

Card # _____

Exp Date Signature _____

Name _____

Address _____

City/State _____

Zip _____

Phone _____

Email _____

Qty.	Title	Total

Subtotal _____

Postage ($4.00 first book; $1.00 each additional;
Order 4 or more books, FREE SHIPPING) _____

Total _____